# Staying Strong

# Staying Strong

## ROBIN McBRYDE

### WITH LYNN DAVIES

*yLolfa*

First impression: 2007

© Copyright Robin McBryde & Y Lolfa Cyf., 2007

The publishers with to acknowledge the financial support of
Cyngor Llyfrau Cymru

Cover design: Y Lolfa
Back cover photograph: Huw Evans Agency, Caerdydd

ISBN: 978 086243 992 7

Published, printed and bound in Wales
by Y Lolfa Cyf., Talybont, Ceredigion SY24 5AP
*website* www.ylolfa.com
*email* ylolfa@ylolfa.com
*tel* 01970 832 304
*fax* 832 782

# In memory of
# John McBryde (1945-2007)

The true meaning of life is to plant trees under whose shade you do not expect to sit.

**Nelson Henderson**

# Introduction

WHEN Y LOLFA, the Welsh publishing company, first asked me early in 2006 whether I'd like to write my autobiography my first reaction was to doubt whether there would be much interest in a book about a retired rugby hooker from north Wales. Yet the more I thought about the matter I realised that it was perhaps *because* I came from a comparatively unfashionable area, as far as top-class rugby in Wales is concerned, that I should consider putting pen to paper.

Having said that, had the original request been for an autobiography in English, I still would have declined. Coming from a Welsh-speaking background where Welsh was, and still is, my first language, it is a much more natural and comfortable process for me to express my views and experiences through the medium of Welsh. I also believe that it is important for Welsh-speaking sports stars, who are often an inspiration to many young people in Wales, to support and undertake themselves the provision of reading material in the Welsh language, particularly in view of the availability of an abundance of similar English-language material.

Nevertheless, following the publication of my Welsh language autobiography, *Y Cymro Cryfa*, in November 2006, I was approached by many non-Welsh-speaking friends and colleagues who told me they would have really liked to know what I had to say about various matters and events in that book. Others kindly mentioned that they had been given to understand that the book was of great interest to followers of rugby in Wales and beyond and that it should be translated into English. As a result of such comments I present *Staying Strong*, which, in addition to including the material found in *Y Cymro Cryfa*, also records my thoughts and experiences as a coach during the past fifteen months.

On a personal note, during this period I also lost my greatest supporter and best friend when my father passed away in June. Having had some time to reflect, I have now been able to write about the feelings and emotions that I felt at the time surrounding his death. However, I haven't yet had the time to reflect on the sad, sudden death of Ray Gravell.

Having written the introduction to *Y Cymro Cryfa*, Ray was due to do likewise for this book. However, although I refer to his illness in the book, I think it appropriate that I take this opportunity to give him a special mention. Reading and listening to the tributes in the days following the news of Ray's death, it becomes evident how much of an influence he had on so many people throughout his career as a rugby player, actor and broadcaster. I had the pleasure of being in Ray's company many times, usually in a rugby environment, but one of the most recent occasions was when I was preparing to stand in for him at the National Eisteddfod as sword bearer. During what must have been a difficult time for Ray and his family, following the amputation of his leg, the support that he gave me was unquestionable. The genuine pride and delight that he expressed towards me when I accepted the honour of carrying the sword was not lost upon me, and I was left in no doubt as to how much it meant to him. To me, he represented all that was good about Wales and always carried all things Welsh with him wherever he went. Ray was indeed a special man, one whom I was privileged to have as a friend and one who always left me with a smile on my face.

I have been able to gain a huge amount of satisfaction from my involvement in rugby, firstly as a player and now as a coach. I also count myself extremely lucky to have had so much enjoyment during my career, especially when I hear of incidents of players sustaining serious injuries on the rugby field. Unfortunately, that's what happened to Bryan Davies, a long-serving member of *Clwb Rygbi'r Bala* (Bala Rugby Club), and a recipient of every honour the club could offer. After playing in the front row for 19 years, and running the mini-rugby section almost single-handed at the club, Bryan decided to hang up his playing boots. He announced his decision in the dressing room prior to the final game of the 2006-7 season and was promptly and rightly made captain for the day. Very early in the game fate took over; the first scrummage ended up as an untidy affair with Bryan prostrate on the floor. Those few seconds changed his life, and that of his wife Sue and young children Ilan and Teleri, for ever. Sadly, current prognosis indicates that Bryan will be paralysed and disabled with a broken neck for the rest of his days. Since that tragic incident his family and friends, as well as the club, have been very active in promoting the Bryan Davies Appeal Fund to raise monies to facilitate his adjustment to his present circumstances. In buying this book you will be making a small contribution to the fund, as all the royalty proceeds that I would normally have received from the sale of this book will be donated to the Bryan Davies Appeal.

To donate to the Bryan Dvaies Appeal Fund, please send to:

'CRONFA APÊL BRYAN DAVIES APPEAL FUND' at the Bala Branch of HSBC BANK

SORT CODE 40 – 09 – 01, Account No. 71234803

ROBIN MCBRYDE
November 2007

# CHAPTER ONE

# Stepping Out

There are only two lasting bequests we can give our children.
One is roots the other wings.

**Hodding Carter**

I HAD NO interest whatsoever in rugby as a boy growing up in Llanfechell, a village in the northernmost part of Anglesey where Welsh was the spoken language and which is located as far from Cardiff as you can get whilst still in Wales. At that time in my life I wouldn't have been able to name a single famous rugby player or rugby club for that matter. The main sporting interest in those parts was soccer and I was a staunch Liverpool supporter, where my great hero, Kenny Dalgleish, was a star. I remember supporting Brazil in the World Cup and going to the trouble of having the names of each of the team's players inscribed on my precious football, but they didn't last very long! At every opportunity, my mates, Alun Lloyd, Stephen Bach, John Tîn and Dei Post and me would bring the fervour of Anfield to the little patch of land beside the swings in the playing field in the middle of the village.

My mother, a native of Llanfechell, and my father, John, who hailed from Corris in Merioneth, began their teaching careers in Anglesey. Perhaps it was no coincidence that I was keen on sport since my father had trials in goal for Cardiff City and played rugby for North Wales as part of a successful back row with the brothers Tony (who eventually played for Wales and became national Coach) and David Gray. He was also a keen cricketer and represented Anglesey as a fast bowler. My mother taught physical education, specialising in dance and my younger sisters,

Naomi and Beth, both share her interest in that respect. They won many competitions, even in England, and Naomi succeeded in obtaining a scholarship to enable her to have ballet lessons at the Royal Ballet in London every Saturday morning for four years. The weekly journey there and back from Bangor called for considerable dedication, from both her and my mother! Naomi is by now a busy mother of two children and Beth is head of drama at a secondary school in London.

When I look back on my early days in Llanfechell, the memory which I cherish most is the freedom we were given to wander wherever we wished and to enjoy the country life, in the company of friends. Helping with the hay, carrying bales and loading trailers on some of the local farms, walking to Cemaes Bay (which would take us two hours, but that's what made it fun), diving into the sea from the pier and exploring the beach, jumping across streams to see who would be the first one to fall in and racing on our bikes like banshees along the narrow country lanes. Happy days! As were my schooldays at Llanfechell Junior School. My Nain (Gran) was the one who used to represent the family at the Sports Day and the school concerts with me, since she cared for us when my parents were at work. In recent years it was so nice to be invited back to the village on two separate occasions to open firstly the local fête and then an extension to the school building. The Sunday School at Jerusalem Chapel also played an important part in my upbringing but often the journey there in the purple Austin driven by Miss Jones, the old lady who lived next door, was more memorable than what I was taught after arriving there!

When I was eight years old we moved to Treborth, near the Menai Straits, which separate Anglesey from mainland Wales. My father had been made Headmaster at Cae Top Primary School in Bangor nearby, and my mother had also been appointed Head of Physical Education at the new Tryfan Secondary School there, which specialised in Welsh-medium teaching. This change led to my very first introduction to rugby when my father began taking me to Treborth School playing fields on Saturday mornings where the Headmaster, Wil Parry Williams, had started mini-rugby sessions, with the help of Meic Griffiths (who subsequently had a huge influence on my development as a player) and Gareth Roberts. At the time Wil was Chairman of Menai Bridge Rugby Club and the weekly sessions proved to be the beginning of a lasting friendship with him and his son Trystan. In those mini-rugby sessions no importance was attached to playing in particular positions. I tended to line up in the backs and took particular pleasure in tackling (my father had given me a little private coaching in that aspect!).

By now I was a pupil at Cae Top Primary School and I expected to be given a lot of stick by my fellow pupils because my father was Headmaster. However this didn't turn out to be the case, mainly, perhaps, because my father didn't actually teach, apart from taking physical education, so I didn't come across him very often. But he was responsible for games and since the school didn't have a blade of grass growing on the site, being completely surrounded by concrete, the only game played there was football. We had a school team, of which I was a member, until we lost 16–0 to Glanadda, a neighbouring school. At that point the Headmaster decided that the school would no longer have a football team, but, rather, a rugby team! Therefore we would have to walk to the University playing fields nearby whenever we wanted to practice so that we could do so with soft ground underfoot. Nevertheless football was still my favourite game and, following a few trial matches, I was chosen for the Bangor and District Primary Schools soccer team. The highlight of that era was a trip to Merseyside to play against a team from Liverpool and, better still, being taken to Goodison to watch Everton play. Not quite as good as watching Liverpool at Anfield perhaps, but for a nine-year-old boy from Treborth it was an unforgettable thrill to see a First Division match live, as opposed to sitting in front of the television.

Yet rugby continued to appeal to me. As a result of the mini-rugby sessions at Treborth I was chosen to represent Bangor and District Primary Schools at rugby and in my first game I soon realised how unfair the comments of spectators on the touchline can be. Early in the game, when I held back a little before falling on the ball in defence, I heard this voice bellowing at me in Welsh, "You look like a sack of potatoes!" To make matters worse I realised that the irate supporter was my father and he was reprimanded by the referee, Dewi Miles, for his comments (although my father swore that he didn't direct any such remark at his dear little boy!). The team also went on a memorable trip to Bedlinog in the Rhymney Valley to play in the D C Thomas Cup Competition. (It is still held today and on more than one occasion during my time with the Scarlets I had the pleasure of meeting some of the teams from North Wales who had travelled South to play in that competition. It was always nice to be able to take them on a tour of Stradey and to introduce them to some of the Llanelli players.) When we arrived at Bedlinog most of the pitch was under water following heavy rain, but since we had travelled such a long way for the game we were allowed to play ten minutes each way, which resulted in our losing by one try to nil. We stayed in the homes of our opponents and that was the first time that I had been away overnight without my parents. However, that in itself wasn't the highlight of the trip for me, but the very tasty faggots and peas, which we were given at the Bedlinog Clubhouse after the game. This was a completely new dish for us North Walians at the time, but over the years I came to realise that it was an essential part of the diet in rugby clubs in the South and I soon acquired a taste for it.

Although the academic side of school life never appealed to

me I have always been interested in music. As a boy in Llanfechell I took piano lessons until I was 14 years old. I then gave them up and have regretted my decision ever since, but I soon turned my attention to another instrument, the trombone, which gave me great pleasure until I left secondary school. I was a member of the County Orchestra and Menai Bridge Brass Band for many years. I had a lot of fun as a band member, under the baton of Dennis Williams, taking part in concerts and competitions in places as far a field as Preston. Unfortunately my musical interests at present are confined to listening to music of a fairly wide spectrum, although Tina, my wife, recently bought me a guitar which I'm determined to master in the near future.

Towards the end of my time in primary school we moved back to Anglesey to the village of Menai Bridge. I chose to go to Tryfan School in Bangor, where my mother taught, but fortunately this proved to be no embarrassment to me either, since she spent the whole of her time teaching the girls.

I was never very happy at Tryfan, mainly because of the unsatisfactory relationship which I had with most of the teachers there. I am prepared to accept that I was mostly to blame for this situation, but not entirely. I often used to display a rebellious streak towards those in authority and that, more than likely, is what later led to Kevin Bowring, when he was national coach, to describe me as 'anti-establishment' in his analysis of the players under his supervision at the time. Even so, I had a very good relationship with some of the teachers, such as Richie Haines, the PE master, who was also in charge of rugby, and Elfyn Roberts, who taught Craft, Design and Technology and also assisted with rugby activities. The reason for this was, I suppose, that they taught subjects which I really enjoyed and I was consequently able to identify with their aspirations. Apart from these two particular subjects and Welsh, I had no interest whatsoever in education while I was a pupil at Tryfan.

I played for the school rugby teams in the various age categories but with no great enthusiasm and without any particular flair for the game. At that time there was an ongoing dispute between teachers and local authorities concerning after-school pursuits, which led, to my great disappointment, to a significant cut in coaching activities in sporting areas such as rugby and in the playing of matches outside normal school hours. Nevertheless this did nothing to dampen the enthusiasm of Richie Haines and I, along with the other pupils, benefited from his love for the game. I was by this time playing as flanker but the only real insight I had into the demands of that particular position was being aware of where I should pack down in the scrum. By this time, too, I had other conflicting interests. I competed for the school in gymnastics, basketball and cricket. I was also chess champion on one occasion but the school could claim no credit for that achievement.

By this time I was really looking forward to leaving school as soon as possible. I passed eight subjects in my GCSE exams and six at the Higher Education Certificate level, including Craft, Design and Technology, before going for an interview for an apprenticeship by Manweb (now known as Scottish Power) as a result. I cannot remember much about the occasion but I was given some special advice beforehand by John Howard Hughes, a family friend, which has stayed with me to this day. He told me that, when being introduced to Manweb officials, I should shake hands very firmly and once only. Even now, I still shake hands in that way but, of course, I have a slightly stronger grip than when I was a boy, with the result that some people actually wince when I greet them. I can honestly say that this is not intentional on my part to be 'macho', but it has simply become an integral part of my being.

That particular advice must have paid off because Manweb offered me an apprenticeship. So, at sixteen years of age, I ventured out to the wide world to receive training as an overhead linesman, with responsibility for erecting and maintaining electricity cables. However, before starting in my new job I was required to pass one important practical test. I had to climb to the top of a high pole with the aid of a harness, and then lean back, with the harness taking the strain, while one of the company instructors shook and rocked the pole like fury!

In the early days I, the little apprentice, was the general dogsbody for Chris Powell, Edgar, Ellis, Keith Bach and Dic Pentrefelin. Every morning Dic would greet me with the words "Got any money?" for he was very partial to a game of pool and a pint at lunchtime. Amongst my other duties were checking oil levels, making sure that there was enough water in the tea jug (although I never took to their liking for boiling the water and the tea together in the jug for their early morning cuppa and then leaving the brew to stew in the jug ready for lunchtime!), and making sure that there were cakes for Hefin and John Charles to accompany their tea. I had been conscientiously providing them with cakes for ages before discovering that they had never been accustomed in the past to such a luxury with their cuppa. It was their way of teasing the new apprentice. Yet I had noticed at the very beginning that cakes made a significant contribution to the well-being of certain members of the gang. For example, Alun Rowlands, the foreman, who was a large man stuffed into a small Metro, would drive me around the area so that I would become acquainted with the local geography. However, he would usually plan his route to coincide with the location of the best cake shops in the vicinity!

Before long, I was really enjoying my work in the open air, which was such a change from my miserable existence at school. I took delight in getting to know the local countryside, in getting to grips with physical tasks, such as digging holes and raising poles, and in absorbing the technical instruction I was getting at the company's training centre in Hoylake (which entailed following courses there for periods of three months at a time for a few years). Above all else I was really enjoying being part of the fun and camaraderie, which existed in the gang. I've kept in touch with some of the lads and we get a chance every so often to re-live those happy times. One of them, Robin Jones, regularly gave me his support over the years by frequently travelling from Anglesey to Stradey to see me play.

When I first went to Hoylake I had to have a medical examination and I was taken aback to discover that I weighed quite a bit more than I should have (although this was based purely on how tall I was). This realisation led to a radical change in the way I regarded my health and the condition of my body. I even began to weigh the Rice Krispies I ate for breakfast each morning, while my grandmother became even more concerned than me about the contents of the food box which she prepared for me each morning to take to work. I began to jog two or three times a week along the roads of Bangor and Menai Bridge in an effort to get my body into a more acceptable state. I also made regular use of the small gym at Treborth School thanks to the cooperation of Wil Parry Williams.

By that time some friends, Irfon Williams, Alan Owen and Andrew Williams and myself, had decided to join the successful Bangor Youth Rugby Team. They regularly played against notable opponents from England, such as Birkenhead Park, New Brighton, Doncaster, Widnes and Orrel and at that time they had just been voted Youth Team of the Year by *Rugby World and Post*. However, since I was only sixteen years of age at the time and playing in the Under 19 age group, I spent most of my time on the bench. I was given an occasional game as a flanker but by my second season at Bangor I sometimes had to play in the front row. I was chosen as tight head prop for a game against Sale, which promised to be quite a volatile confrontation since both teams were unbeaten at that point. There was quite a bit of niggle in the match which led me to purposely clashing heads with the opposing loose head when going in to a scrum. They were obviously used to dealing with such behaviour, and the Sale hooker started biting my ear while their loose head let go some sledgehammer blows to my face. "Welcome to the front row!' was the message. It was an important lesson for a young inexperienced scrummager, namely if you're inclined to start trouble you must always be fully prepared for the backlash!

That night, owing to the attention given to me by the Sale front row, I had to go to the local hospital, Ysbyty Gwynedd, for a medical examination. While I was there I came across Meic Griffiths, who used to take me for mini-rugby sessions at Treborth and who was by this time the coach of Menai Bridge Rugby Club. With him was Carl Jones, a former playing colleague from the early days, who was now playing in the Menai Bridge front row. At the time I wasn't too happy with my lot at Bangor Rugby Club, mainly because the coach, for some reason, had taken half the boys that had won the Youth Team of theYear Award with him to Llangefni Rugby Club to establish a youth team there. At the hospital Meic and Carl asked me to consider joining Menai Bridge Youth Team. The Menai Bridge Club was ten years old at that time and played in the Gwynedd League. It had already proved to be one of the most successful clubs in north Wales for developing local talent since, for example, Arthur Emyr, Iwan Jones and Stuart Roy – all of whom had represented Wales at senior level – started their senior rugby careers there. I accepted the invitation to join the club, a decision that led to a period when I could honestly say that I really enjoyed playing rugby for the very first time in my life. Things began to click for me at Menai Bridge and under Meic's coaching a very promising team came together.

Joining Menai Bridge was also the catalyst for getting my

body into even better shape for the harsh demands of the front row. I came to depend on two people for whom I had the utmost respect and whose assistance during that time I value greatly to this day. The first is Elvie Parry, whose career as hooker with Menai Bridge was drawing to a close when I arrived. He was my first ever rugby hero. He had this unusual way of wearing his headband on the rugby field, allowing the two straps on either side of the head to remain untied during the game so that they trailed in the breeze behind him, creating a Rambo-like effect as he charged around the pitch! So I decided that I would adopt the same style of headband when I was playing.

Elvie was a weight lifter who kept the necessary equipment for this pursuit in a shed at his home. Carl and I would go there to work out, under Elvie's instruction, about twice a week, which would leave us bathed in sweat, even in mid-winter, although there was no heating there. I remember that, after my very first session, my arms were too weak to turn the car's steering wheel during the journey home! I don't know whether the old shed is still standing, but when I recall the rusty nails that attached the equipment to the woodwork and the huge strain on everything there, I have my doubts. As well as developing me physically, these sessions challenged me psychologically. They were always competitive and made you work until literally you could give no more. We did sometimes overstep the mark however, and on one occasion in particular when Elvie and I went biking from Menai Bridge through the Llanberis Pass and back, I got home and had to see a doctor simply because I was completely dehydrated. Despite that unfortunate experience I'm still greatly indebted to Elvie who without doubt helped me in my mental approach to hard work.

The other person at the Club who had a great influence on me was Meic. Although he held regular weekly training sessions with the team he would go out of his way, during his spare time, to give me and a few friends, such as Huw Percy, Carl and Trystan, extra coaching on basic skills and fitness. During the early days he was my guru on matters concerning fitness and we still keep in touch to this day.

After a few weeks playing for Menai Bridge Youth I was quite fit. As well as going to the weekly team-training sessions I was also by this time working out on my own three nights a week. That meant that I was enjoying my rugby so much more and, for the first time in my career as a player, I was getting particular pleasure from feeling that I was better than those who were playing against me. During my second season at Menai Bridge I was made captain of the youth team. I really enjoyed the experience and was particularly pleased that I was selected to play for the North Wales Youth team. The enemy at that time, at least as far as Menai Bridge supporters were concerned, was Llangefni Youth and I remember, when we met in the Gwynedd Cup, my father, Wil and others cursing on one touch line while Meic, in his usual quiet way had disassociated himself from such comments and had withdrawn to the other side of the field. Yet he was as pleased as anyone that we won that game and also another against Llangefni in a seven-a-side tournament in Rhyl at the end of that season. On that occasion I remember a Llangefni player's mother shouting at me, "If you were my son I would kill you!" To which I replied, "If you were my mother I would probably kill myself!" which seemed an appropriate response at the time!

Since I was now eighteen years old I also began playing for the Menai Bridge senior team. Yet I realised that I was still pretty raw as far as the techniques of playing hooker were concerned. For example, because I hadn't, as yet, learned how to support the weight in the scrum, in order that I might raise my right leg to hook the ball, I would get the ball back by literally using my head. While I also got to grips with the technique required to throw the ball into the line I remember being amazed to learn from one of the lads in the team that Alan Phillips, the Wales hooker at the time, and Robert Norster, the pack's main jumper, had devised a special code to determine whether Norster should move forward or back to take the ball when the hooker threw it into the line. How ingenious, I thought! But I must have made some progress by the end of that season since the club chose me as Youth Player of the Year and also Senior Team Player of the Year.

By this time rugby was central to my life and, in addition to the pleasure I got from playing, I really enjoyed the fun and the camaraderie that were such a part of the rugby scene, especially in the company of other members of the front row brotherhood such as Rich Tom (who, on the recent approach of his fiftieth year, continued to play for Menai Bridge, in the same team as his son), and Gwyn Banc, who also played alongside his son and who continues to turn out for the team from time to time, despite being in his mid-fifties. Those were the two props who had the task of supporting me in my first ever game at senior level. The Club had many other characters, like Glyn Gough, Robin Phillips, Gags, Davy Crocket, Alan Clarke, Doug Barnes, Neil Patrick and Carl, all of whom ensured that those early days in my playing career were indeed memorable. I still keep in touch with the club and I was greatly honoured to be invited, a few years ago, to officially open their new field and clubhouse on the very edge of the Menai Straits, surely one of the most picturesque locations of all the rugby clubs in Wales. I know that many people have worked relentlessly to establish the new club and I was particularly pleased for Wil Parry Williams who was by then President and who had given such a lot of his time and energy to ensure the success of Menai Bridge Rugby Club.

During the 1988-89 season, when I was 19 years old, I was selected to represent the North Wales Under 23 team, coached by Denley Isaac, who became one of the main influences on my playing career. He was himself a former hooker, was the coach at Mold Rugby Club and also assisted in coaching the Wales Under 21 team. Denley suggested that perhaps I would benefit as a player from joining Mold, who played at a higher level than Menai Bridge, thereby giving me the opportunity possibly of playing against first-class clubs from time to time. Therefore, early in the 1989-90 season, I decided to leave Menai Bridge Rugby Club (later joined by my friend, the prop Carl Jones) for Mold Rugby Club, a move which proved to be the beginning of an eventful period in my development as a player.

# CHAPTER 2

# Mold and Beyond

Be daring, be different, be impractical, be anything that will
assert integrity of purpose and imaginative vision against the
play-it-safers, the creatures of the commonplace, the slaves of
the ordinary.

**Sir Cecil Beaton**

DURING MY FIRST game for Mold against Sandbach I began
to think that, by changing clubs in order to play at a
higher level, I had, maybe, bitten off more than I could chew.
The comments of some of the supporters certainly seemed to
suggest that, according to some of the comments my father
overheard that afternoon.

*"No wonder we're losing, we haven't got a hooker!"*

*"Who's this new hooker then?"*

*"Never mind, he won't be playing next week!"*

And that was indeed the case since I was dropped to the
second team the following Saturday. But my performances soon
improved as I was now getting specific and regular coaching
from Denley, sometimes on such basic scrummaging aspects as
the positioning of my feet and the angle of my body. In addition
I had very experienced players alongside me and in due course
the thought of playing against renowned clubs such as New
Brighton, for example, didn't bother me at all. Indeed the Mold
club had this general air of professionalism about it. Little
touches, such as, for example, meeting up with the rest of the
team for lunch at a local hotel before walking over to the Club to
play an important fixture, made a great impression on me. Yet it
was obvious that I was very slow to impress the local press, for

in match reports on one or two of my early games I was referred to as Robin Munroe and Robin McGuire.

Yet playing for Mold was not all roses since it took over an hour to travel there, all the way from Menai Bridge in Anglesey, where we now lived as a family. There were twice-weekly training sessions to attend, usually after a hard day's work and with no time for a meal before setting off. My father was my chauffeur in the early days and that in it self was a cause of some embarrassment. For while we were training on a nearby pitch he would sit in his car in the club car park trying to catch up on some reading or marking, despite the poor lighting. At the end of one of our sessions one of the lads came into the changing rooms and announced, "That ****ing pervert is out there watching us again tonight, boys!" Since I was the reticent new boy I didn't say a word at the time, but before long I had introduced Dad to the officials and, from then on, he was able to avail himself of the club facilities in comfort while waiting for me.

While I was in my first year with Mold I was invited to train with the Wales Under 20 team in Cardiff, mainly perhaps because Denley was part of the coaching set-up there. It was quite a journey from Anglesey, bearing in mind that the training sessions were usually held on Sunday mornings (following my usual game with Mold on the Saturday). So my father would take me down to Cardiff by car after the match and we would stay in a hotel on Cathedral Road. The team would train throughout the Sunday then we would both jump in the car to travel almost 200 miles back to Menai Bridge on the Sunday evening. Sometimes I had to travel down to an evening session midweek, straight after work, and still have to be back in the yard at Llangefni in time for the following morning's duties. I must have made some kind of impression in Cardiff for I was chosen to play in one of the final trial matches for the Wales Under 20 team, to be held at Treherbert. I remember getting the fright of my life that day when I saw the Rhondda Valley for the first time. As the car descended along the mountain road from the direction of Hirwaun, I was amazed at this panorama of endless terraces below me, which seemed to stretch as far as the eye could see. I got to the rugby field and was even more astonished to find that it had a huge fence around it – to keep people out!

At that particular stage of my development I looked quite fit, and the work that I had been doing with Elvie and Meic was evident in my physique, to the extent that I had to make a slit under the arm pits of my trial shirt so that I could get into it. I also remember Denley's advice on how I should set about making an impression on the chief coach at the time, Kevin Bowring. Namely that I should make sure that, when I was exchanging shirts during half time, I did so under Mr Bowring's very nose, so that he couldn't fail to notice my form! One of the second rows that night was Derwyn Jones, who measured 6' 10" in his stockinged feet, who apparently expressed his displeasure with my throwing into the line that night. My father, however, was furious with him, being of the opinion that Derwyn wasn't bothering to jump at all, but was happy simply to raise his arms. Dad had probably got things wrong again. In any event I got into the team, to play against the Breconshire Under 23 side. We lost the match, 9–22, despite having a few stars of the future in our side, such as Rob Howley, Mike Voyle, David Llewellyn and Derwyn.

The 1990-91 season was quite disappointing for Mold. We did, however, manage one achievement, which impressed many rugby aficionados. In the fourth round of the Schweppes Cup we came within a hair's breadth of beating Cross Keys, one of the first-class clubs in Wales at that time. The final score was 7–12 but, considering that no club from North Wales had ever beaten a team of that standard, we were very proud of our performance. The game served as a milestone for me for more than one reason. Firstly, although I was just 19 years old, and had many experienced players alongside me, I was chosen to lead the pack for that game, something which I considered to be a great honour. Secondly, with the aid of our experienced tighthead prop, Roger Bold, their two best hookers, David Basham and Paul Jones, were forced to leave the field, one of whom thought that he had broken his jaw, as a result of the pressure we were able to exert on their front row. It was that particular match that led me to believe, for the very first time, that maybe I had a future at the highest level of the game.

Shortly after that encounter I represented North Wales against Gwent in Wrexham, and, during the opening period, I got such a fierce smack in the mouth that one of my front teeth became loose. So I pulled it out and threw it to Denley, asking him to look after it until the final whistle. The famous Charlie Faulkner, one of the Gwent coaches, standing beside Denley at the time, asked:

*"What did 'e just throw to you?"*

*"His front tooth,"* was Denley's reply.

*"You must all be bloody mad up 'ere!"* said Charlie, shaking his head in disbelief.

Perhaps he'd heard of the recent problems we had caused the hookers in Cross Keys. But in one respect he was right because, for the rest of the game, I had to run about the field with my mouth firmly closed since, even if the slightest breath of air reached the hole where the tooth had once been, an excruciating pain shot through my head. I had to wear a plate in my mouth to compensate for that particular loss, and it would occasionally find its way to the bottom of a fellow player's pint glass on a Saturday night!

During this period the former renowned All Black scrum-half, Sid Going, brought the New Zealand Under 21 team to Wales and I played against them for the North Wales Under 23 team at Rhyl. We drew 16–16, and I took great pleasure from the fact that we'd exerted a lot of pressure on the opposition's front row. As a result I was chosen for the Wales President's XV Under 21 squad against the New Zealand Under 21 team. Also in our squad were Neil Jenkins, Rob Howley, Paul John and Scott Gibbs, who unfortunately had to withdraw because of injury. The first-choice hooker was Andrew Lamerton who had already represented the Llanelli first team against the full All Blacks team, so it was no surprise that he started the game. We played really well and won the game 34–13, with Neil kicking 14 points. I got a chance to make an appearance during the second half and took pride in the fact that our front row continued to give the opposing front row a hard time. On that particular day I was the only member of the Welsh squad who had no affiliation with a first-class club, and although I didn't feel that there was any significant difference between myself and the rest of the boys with regard to fitness and the general standard of play, I was, however, aware that the others had some advantage over me in the way they were able to adapt their basic skills to specific aspects of the game. Funnily enough I've noticed the same deficiencies in the play of some of the boys who come down from North Wales to train down South. One other way in which perhaps I differed from the other boys in the Welsh team was that I kept every official letter that I received from the WRU, even letters informing me of training sessions with the Welsh Under 20 team, maybe because I wasn't able to believe, without that official confirmation, that these things had happened to me.

When we were in the showers after the New Zealand game in Pontypridd, Ron Waldron, the Welsh team coach at the time, who'd been an excellent prop in his day, called to congratulate the team. As he passed by he told me that, in his opinion, I should move to play in South Wales if I wanted to succeed in the game. I went back to Mold and mentioned this conversation to Denley, who fully agreed with Ron Waldron. The more I thought about it the greater my desire to give it a go. I felt that I would carry on living in the same place, playing the same standard of rugby, forever perhaps, unless I joined one of the first-class clubs in south Wales.

Because of his links with the Wales Under 21 team Denley had connections with the Cardiff, Glamorgan Wanderers and Swansea clubs, so he made enquiries on my behalf. Swansea had, apparently, been watching me, and in December 1990, at the end of one of the Under 20 fitness training sessions in Cardiff, one of the Whites' coaches, Alan Lewis from Ystradgynlais (who was covered in coal dust having dashed over to Cardiff as soon as he'd finished his shift in the local coal mine), turned up with a piece of paper in his hand and asked me to sign for Swansea Rugby Club. I'd already heard that Cardiff had an experienced hooker called Ian Watkins (although the name meant nothing to me) and that the Swansea hooker, Billy James, was coming to the end of his career, so I signed for the Whites that very afternoon. There was no mention of terms or conditions or anything else. What was important for me was that I was now a Swansea Rugby Club player.

Sometime after leaving the Mold club, during a conversation I had with one or two of my fellow players there, it was put to me that I'd looked upon my period with them, from the very beginning, as a stepping stone towards bigger things. I was amazed to hear this because there was absolutely no truth in that suggestion. When I joined them my only aim had been to play rugby at a higher level than the one to which I had been accustomed in order to improve my game. I hadn't thought for a minute, when I became a Mold player, that I had a future beyond that particular level. But as a result of the coaching I got at Mold and particularly following the experience I gained playing against teams of a higher standard, I began to think that maybe there was a chance that I could move up a level by playing in south Wales. I enjoyed my time at Mold immensely and I was loath to leave. It had also one quality, which was so rare amongst other clubs at that level, namely the professional manner in which it looked after its players. For example, after I fractured a bone in my foot during a club game everything was handled on my behalf, including insurance payments and surgery, for which I was very grateful. I am greatly indebted to the club and in particular to individuals like Denley, and Dick Jones who was President at the time.

Before signing for Swansea I had already succeeded in getting a job with the South Wales Electricity Company (SWALEC), doing the same kind of work as I did with Manweb in Anglesey. I was based in Glyn Taff near Pontypridd and I thought that living and working in the Rhondda would be fairly convenient, whichever rugby club I would eventually join. In that respect one of the SWALEC staff happened to mention that one of his relatives was looking for a lodger, so I arranged, after my parents had given the OK, to stay with Susan Harries at 54 Parry Street, Ton Pentre. I spent two very happy years there and, although I was supposed to rent just one room, I had the run of the house, and also benefited from her mother Connie's Sunday lunches.

From my experience in the Rhondda I felt that the people there accept strangers directly into their community or society much more readily than we do in north Wales. We, perhaps, are initially more wary, and take a little longer before we're able to make people feel at home. It was easy, therefore, for me to settle in Ton Pentre and be accepted by my workmates. Yet I found that they weren't quite so industrious as the Anglesey gang. We were supposed to start work at eight o'clock in Glyn Taff but it was more like half past eight by the time everybody had arrived at the yard, having had to squeeze through the parked cars that lined both sides of the streets along the way and been given their assignments for the day. Then the first task was to agree on a café in order to discuss the work schedule for the day. There were a few to choose from, but the favourite was the Cil' Café in Cilfynydd, where we would also put the world of rugby in order. As far as their attitude towards me was concerned, playing for Swansea was all right but for someone like Howard Jones, one of the characters in the gang and a fervent Pontypridd supporter, the greatest sin anyone could commit on this earth was to support Cardiff, or even worse, play for them!

Despite the daily temptation to indulge in the very tasty cooked full breakfast which the Cil' Café provided for the gang, I had become accustomed to providing my own food for breakfast and lunch, ever since my early days in the Llangefni yard, and it was very difficult to break with that habit, but I did treat myself on a few occasions, and even finished the breakfast off with the odd cream cake! I spent very many happy hours there and I often recall the fun that was to be had in the company of Peter and Julie, who ran the café, and the gang as they put the world to rights. The same family even today runs the café and we still exchange Christmas cards.

With regard to my daily work schedule I was placed in the care of a great character called Viv Hext, a short man who was wide in stature and who sported a thick moustache. He epitomised the welcome in the Rhondda, and 'took me under his wing', so to speak. He was single minded in many ways but very likeable and memories of him still make me smile. Although he passed away some time ago I'm still in touch with his widow, Fay, who lives in Ynysybwl, near Pontypridd. He had one big fault however... wherever there was dog mess, Viv would be sure to tread on it and carry it unknowingly on his shoes. He spoiled many a nice carpet, fouled many a clean floor and caused many a stink in houses the length and breadth of the Rhondda. But, worse for me, after he'd stepped in the dog mess, he would often have cause to climb a ladder while attending to his work... and whose job was it to carry the ladder on his shoulder when the job was finished? You're right, muggings! Fortunately for me, a third member, a young apprentice by the name of Stuart Howe, joined us so I could at least share the responsibility.

There were quite a few stunts that we pulled on one another, but one which caused me most embarrassment was when I'd be working at the top of a ladder in a confined porch or entrance hall, as was frequently the case in the valley terraced houses. One of the other two would come in and let rip with a fart! The culprit would then open the front door to get out, close it suddenly behind him and ring the doorbell outside, whereupon the householder would naturally hurry to open the entrance hall door in order to get to the front door, at which point he or she would of course be confronted by this awful stench. Since there was only one other person, namely me, present at that time it was perfectly reasonable to think that I was the one responsible for the terrible stink that by now pervaded most of downstairs! Despite (or because of) such stunts that we pulled on one another, the three of us got on like a house on fire and as a result made light work of the most demanding of jobs that were given to us.

I rarely had cause to socialise with the gang outside working hours, except during the summer, once a week, when quite a few of us turned out for the work's cricket team. I played wicket keeper and enjoyed the games very much. Before moving South I'd played for the Bangor Cricket Club's youth team and then for the second eleven. During the rugby season training duties at St. Helens took up two nights a week and most of each weekend and for the remainder of my leisure time I'd concentrate on my personal fitness by going to the gym in Abergorki. I didn't get drawn by the traditional leisure activities in which many of my work colleagues were involved however. One of them, Geoff

Thomas, who would give me a lift to and from work in the back of his painter's van, would regularly call in his local club (there were so many social clubs dotted around the valleys) for a pint and a game of draughts or dominoes. Only then would he go home for tea and change his clothes, but he would then return to the club for more of the same. That's one thing I found to be particularly strange when I first arrived there. The second was that the Welsh language was not to be heard anywhere and during my time there with SWALEC I hardly ever had cause to speak Welsh. On that point I think the gang had quite some difficulty in understanding my Anglesey accent when I spoke English, and I was told on more than one occasion to 'talk tidy, mun'!

Soon after settling in Ton Pentre I was informed by Swansea Rugby Club that training sessions were held on Tuesday and Thursday evenings and that, when I attended for the first time, I should ask for Byron Mugford, a former player who was now one of the club officials. I had a problem however: I'd never been to Swansea, so I had to make lengthy enquiries as to how I was to get there from Ton Pentre. Somehow or other I got to the big city with no great difficulty and since I knew that the St. Helens ground was near the sea, I aimed the little Fiesta in the direction of the Bay, and looked out for the floodlight towers which would indicate that I had arrived. And there they were! I parked near the stadium and walked through an open doorway. There was a man inside doing some maintenance work and when I asked him where I could find Byron Mugford he replied *"Never 'eard of 'im!"* That very instant I noticed that there was a soccer goal, with nets attached, directly behind him. I had, of course, arrived at the Vetch Field, home to the Swans soccer team!

Before long I was back on the road, which ran alongside the Bay and soon spotted another set of floodlights, this time at St. Helens. As I arrived there, I could see Arthur Emyr, one of the Swansea players, getting out of his car, so I parked nearby. I knew Arthur, for he had been brought up about a mile from my home in Menai Bridge and we had both started our senior rugby careers at the same local club, but during different periods. Fortunately he accompanied me to the changing rooms and introduced me to the captain, Robert Jones, and the other players, who included Anthony Clement, Malcolm Dacey, Richard Webster, Paul Arnold, Richard Moriarty, Simon Davies, Mark Wyatt, Keith Colclough and Billy James. I don't remember much about that first training session, since my head was in the clouds and I was continually having to ask myself what the hell I was doing there alongside such an array of stars from the rugby world!

# CHAPTER 3

# The Whites

Obstacles cannot crush me; every obstacle yields to stern resolve.
**Leonardo da Vinci**

WHEN I RAN on to the training ground that first night I was wearing rugby boots that covered the ankle, which weren't exactly trendsetters at the time. Billy James, the first team hooker, took one look at them and said *"You'll 'ave to get rid of those bloody boots for a start!"* He had a quick word with someone on the touchline who was in charge of the kit and in a flash I was the proud owner of brand new boots and a tracksuit. Rugby at the highest level was already beginning to appeal to me.

During those early days with Swansea no one in particular took overall charge of the training sessions being that Alan Lewis had left the club before my arrival. Different aspects of the game were the responsibility of various individuals; for example, Alun Donovan was the backs coach, whereas Trevor Cheeseman took fitness training and he along with Richard Moriarty looked after the forwards. My main problem was adjusting to the pace of the game at that level. Although I was able to hold my own as far as strength and durability were concerned (at the time I was 5' 11" and weighed 16 stone) I wasn't particularly fast and my knowledge of skills and set moves did not match that of my fellow players. Therefore, in the beginning, I tended to concentrate during the training sessions on those particular aspects. For example Richard Moriarty would take me to one side and make me throw the ball at him hard and high, just like I would have to do in a match situation, while he jumped for it, shouting *"Harder! Harder!"* after every throw. Of course the hooker's responsibilities were very different in those days. It was illegal, for example, to lift jumpers in the lineout or for the forwards to move about once it had formed, so the hooker would have just two or possibly three targets to aim at during a game; it was therefore essential to practice hitting those targets regularly. In addition, the lineout system was further complicated in those days by a greater number of illegal tactics.

Richard Moriarty was one of the most streetwise operators in the lineout, but my name would be mud if I failed to find him with my throws during a game. I remember, on more than one occasion during those early days, when the ball would perhaps sail over his head in the line, perhaps owing to some misunderstanding about the call, or due to an error on my part. He would then stand, rooted to the spot (although the rest of the pack would have long gone in pursuit of the ball), place his hands on his hips, glare at me and shout *"What the f\*\*\* was that?"*, while I stood there embarrassed, waiting for the ground to swallow me and feeling two foot high!

I first wore the All Whites shirt as a flanker when I took to the field as a sub against Ebbw Vale. As I sat on the bench for most of the eighty minutes I was struck by the irony of the situation, in that the game was the very first top-class club match that I had ever seen. The following week, however, I was chosen to play hooker against Penarth in a midweek fixture, and although my general play about the pitch had been satisfactory my confidence took quite a blow. I found that I was under much more pressure in the scrum than I had been used to and the opposing hooker took three scrums against the head, a rare occurrence at first-class level. Their experienced front row succeeded in taking me down so low that I was unable to lift my right leg to hook the ball.

The provocative comment I got from the gang in the Cilfynydd Café, when they read about it in the *Western Mail* the following morning, was *"There we are then, you'd better go back to north Wales!"* During the following training session at St Helens my apparent weakness in the scrum was the focus of some discussion, with Billy James giving me advice on how to adjust the position of my legs and feet when under pressure. Things improved in the next game against Cardiff, when I only lost one scrum against the head, and that to Ian Watkins, one of the best hookers in Wales at the time. I still remember his comment when it happened. *"Oh! Unlucky!"* but somehow I don't think it was a heartfelt expression of sympathy on his part!

Surprisingly, perhaps, from my personal experience, hookers had very little time for 'sledging' in the scrum. Maybe the heat of the fiery furnace made it a little too uncomfortable for us to be bothered about giving each other verbal stick. There were a couple of exceptions though, one of them being Mark Regan, who had the ability to talk consistently throughout the game. But the greatest threat to any hooker, although it doesn't happen often nowadays, was always one of the opposite second rows 'sending one through' (aiming a punch) towards you in the scrum. One of my first experiences of this was against Neath when the brothers Glyn and Gareth Llywellyn took to raining a few blows to my face as I packed down in the front row. I had cause to remind Gareth of this a few years later. *"What did you expect?"* he replied with tongue-in-cheek. *"You were buggering up our scrum!"* Perhaps the main reason why this didn't happen that often was that the second rows, not being able to see their target, have been known to strike their own hooker, so practice was required!

Some three months after joining Swansea I scored my first try in top-class rugby, against the Barbarians. Perhaps I would be expected to refer to the event as a very memorable experience. Frankly, I have no recollection of it. In the first instance, although the Barbarians' team was full of stars, their names meant nothing to me; I had played so few first-class games that I knew hardly anything about players from outside Wales. Secondly, although I didn't score that many tries during my career, I derived little satisfaction from doing so. What gave me particular pleasure was charging up field and flattening an opponent or two on the way, with the acknowledgement of the spectators ringing in my ears. These, of course, were aspects of the game, which gave me an opportunity to display my fitness and my strength. In that respect I felt that I could hold my own with the best, but I was prepared to concede that there were still certain deficiencies in my game. My general all-round skills and reading of the game needed to improve, as did my hooking technique. Therefore I continued, at that time, to draw upon Denley's knowledge and experience at Mold Rugby Club in order to try and rectify my faults.

I was enjoying my time with the All Whites both on and off the field and there was a lot of fun to be had with the rest of the boys. Many of them, such as Arthur Emyr, Robert Jones, Mark Titley, Kevin Hopkins, Alan Reynolds and Ian Davies (and late arrivals, Scott Gibbs and Aled Williams) were Welsh speakers like myself, and that was the language we would use when speaking to each other. After the usual Saturday match we would spend a couple of hours in the clubhouse at St. Helens before going up to the city for the rest of the evening. Even when we were playing away we would usually come back to Swansea that evening for our entertainment. Since some of us lived quite a distance from the city, Swansea Rugby Club made a deal with The Dragon, one of the area's nicest hotels, enabling us to stay there on the Saturday night at half price, so I regularly took advantage of that particular offer. Of course, during the summer, when there were no games or training sessions, I rarely had cause to go to Swansea. But I still needed to keep fit, so I made my own arrangements in that respect. I continued to go to the gym at Abergorki and I also joined a local athletics club so that I could make regular use of their running track at Tonyrefail. When I visited north Wales I would, once again, turn to Meic Griffith for assistance in maintaining my fitness and the cricket matches with the lads at work were also helpful in that respect.

Swansea finished third from bottom of the Welsh First-Class Clubs League at the end of 1990-91 and I was looking forward to better things at the beginning of the new season, which would be my first full season at the club. By this time Mike Ruddock had been appointed Coach and Billy James, the regular first team hooker had left. The first new player to be enticed to Swansea by Mike was Garin Jenkins, from Pontypool, who had already played for Wales. Since league regulations prohibited his selection until the end of November, I was selected to play the first two league matches, against Cardiff, when we performed particularly well to win 23–9, and against Neath, when we lost 6–22, following a very disappointing display by our forwards (who succeeded in winning just three lineouts throughout the game!).

From then on Garin was the first choice hooker, but that didn't worry me too much in the beginning since I knew that I still had a lot to learn. Yet I wasn't given much opportunity to draw upon his experience and neither did he, naturally perhaps, go out of his way to try and make me a better hooker. He was desperately keen to play in every game if he could, without any inclination to let an apprentice hooker like me gain some experience. As the season progressed I started to get a bit restless and frustrated since I was hardly ever selected for the first team. As a matter of fact I only played three more league games during the remainder of that season.

I wasn't the only unsettled player; a feeling of 'us and them' took root between the first-team regulars and those who played in the mid-week games. Mike Ruddock didn't seem prepared to experiment with his team at all – we got to think that, injuries aside, he would have liked to put the same fifteen on the field week after week. I remember one occasion during that period, because I was getting so little competitive rugby with Swansea, that I travelled all the way to London for a sevens competition arranged by an old friend of mine, Chris Shears.

Yet I couldn't dispute the fact that the first team was playing exceptionally well and by the beginning of 1992 we were at the top of the League. Players like Scott Gibbs (who scored three tries in his league debut against Cardiff) and Aled Williams had strengthened the squad and there was a greater degree of professionalism apparent in the way the club was being run and in the training methods deployed. Preparatory work for us, the players, was now much more thorough, with Mike Ruddock, in an effort to raise standards, making great use of video equipment, performance charts and personal files on all the players. He would place great emphasis on trying to perfect our play in the tight and would spend time, prior to a game, analysing the playing methods of our opponents and would distribute information sheets on the strengths and weaknesses of various opposition team members.

Not much time would be spent discussing team tactics in the training sessions (or it was my fault for not paying attention!) but there was an ever-increasing emphasis on fitness, with greater use being made of specialised equipment to measure standards. Mike brought in a psychologist, Andy Smith, to the club who would stress to the players, as they listened while lying on the floor, the importance of effective mental imagery, with the basic aim of making them feel better as performers. I can't say that, at the time, I fully appreciated that particular aspect of conditioning players but I came to realise later on that, done properly, it could very well be an effective method. Yet I must confess that I've never been a great fan of psychological tests that call for ticking boxes. It could be argued, however, that one or two players who participated in the training sessions at Swansea needed to see a psychologist, such as Richard Webster and Alan Reynolds, two members of the back row for whom I had the greatest respect. During training sessions their idea of proving how hard and fit they were would be to run at speed directly at each other without taking any evasive action whatsoever and when taking a side-step was seen as 'chickening out'. That sight of the two of them was frightening, and I was glad that they were on my side!

Swansea were Heineken League Champions that season and the boys were looking forward to the club tour to Canada in August. However, personally I was rather apprehensive of flying. Apart from a couple of skiing trips to Europe as a schoolboy my flying experience was very limited and the thought of spending ten hours on a plane to Canada was torture for me. But as it turned out the journey wasn't bad at all and our visit was a very pleasant experience. The team spirit was excellent and we won all three games there, against Alberta, the British Columbia President's XV and the British Columbia team itself, who were champions of Canada at the time. I played in every game, because Garin Jenkins was chosen at tighthead prop for each match as we were short of players in that particular position on the tour. I benefited from the situation since it gave me an opportunity to measure my performance against overseas players of a similar standard and I was happy with the way things went!

Back at Swansea, for the beginning of the 1992-93 season, I had to accept that I was still considered as Garin's understudy. There was one other hooker on the club's books, Lloyd Isaac, from Clyne, near Tonna, in the Neath Valley, who had played for Wales at all levels between the ages of 16 and 21. He was the son of John Isaac, who had himself played hooker for the All Whites between 1961 and 1964. John had been in a similar position to me during his period at St. Helens for he, at that time, competed with Norman Gale, for the hooker's berth. In 1963 Norman eventually joined Llanelli since he'd lost his place to John in the Swansea team.

In 1964 John went on tour with Wales to South Africa, on the occasion of the teams first ever visit there, but he wasn't selected to play in any of the games. Soon after his return he left Swansea to play rugby league with Swinton. He sometimes had cause to visit Stradey to see Lloyd play and although he would often see Norman Gale on such occasions they never once spoke to each other.

During my time with Swansea Lloyd was never given an opportunity to become a serious contender for the hooker's position in that he was such a versatile and talented player that he was often selected to play scrum-half or flanker. Soon after the beginning of the 1993-94 season he decided to join Neath, but not before he'd introduced me, during our socialising sessions as Swansea players, to his sister Tina, who is now my wife, but more of that later. He hadn't been at the Gnoll more than a few weeks before he was selected to play against the touring Australian team, this time as a centre!

Swansea, too, were looking forward to giving Australia a warm welcome at St. Helens and I would have given anything to play against Phil Kearns, the Wallabies hooker, who was considered to be the best in the world in that position at the time. It was no surprise that Garin was selected, but it was still my greatest disappointment as a player up until then. People were constantly reminding me of how far I had progressed in my rugby career in such a short period of time and I fully realised that very many players would have been delighted to exchange places with me on the bench against Australia. However, by this time I was all fired up to play in prestigious games and if I wasn't selected to take the field I didn't really feel that I was part of the set-up. It must also be remembered that it wasn't all that easy for a 'sub' to get to play in those days, since a doctor always had to certify that any player who sought to leave the field did so because he was injured and consequently unable to continue. That particular day was one to remember for the Swansea club since the Wallabies were beaten 21–6 (with Garin getting the winning try) - no mean achievement since Australia proceeded to hammer the Wales team shortly afterwards.

Garin was indeed a character, a former coal miner who was so typical of Rhondda lads in many ways. He liked to tease his fellow players and would always have a funny quip at the ready, often at his own expense. He was the subject of one particular tale, following the Australia game, which lived on in the club for a long time afterwards. He'd decided to provoke Phil Kearns from the very first scrum, so when the two front rows locked together Garin began with *"I'm the Number One, I'm the Number One"*. He continued with this for the next three or four scrums, until Kearns, who by now had tired of Garin's antics, decided to respond to his boast with *"Yeah, the number one shithead more like!"* According to the boys in the pack that day this was the first time they'd been in a scrum that had almost collapsed because it was rocking so much with laughter.

I've always got on well with Garin, despite our rivalry for the hooker's position at club and international level but, in a manner of speaking, it was due to his fiery temperament that I came to the attention of the Wales selectors at the beginning of 1993. I had been selected for the national squad before Christmas and since Garin was sent off in a game between Swansea and Llanelli the following January, he had been suspended for sixteen weeks. As a result I got the chance to play regularly for the Swansea first team but rumour had it, at the time, that Nigel Meek, the

Pontypool hooker, would be first choice for the Wales team that winter.

By now I had left the Rhondda Valley and was working from the SWALEC yard in Llanfihangel-ar-arth, near Llandysul, in Cardiganshire. I had also moved to live in a flat in Capel Dewi, Carmarthenshire, which was owned by the local garage proprietor, Alan Evans. The main reason for my requesting a transfer to work in that particular part of the country was to cut down on the time I spent travelling to Swansea and back for training sessions and matches. But other factors had influenced my decision, such as the desire to speak Welsh. I had been keen to move to somewhere where I could live my daily life at work and at home primarily speaking Welsh. For that very reason, during my time in the Rhondda Valley, I had for the first time ever begun listening to cassettes of Dafydd Iwan (a very popular Welsh singer) and even those of male voice choirs!

Nevertheless I had my regrets when I left Ton Pentre. I was given a great send-off by the gang in 'The Rob' social club in Ynysybwl and, at the end of the night, they formed a circle around me to sing '*I Long to See the Rhondda Once Again*', a song made famous by a local singer, David Alexander. It was a very emotional occasion for I had spent two very happy years in their company. I had arrived there as a young boy at a time when I sorely missed my friends and family in north Wales, not knowing whether I would be able to settle in the south at all. But it wasn't long before the welcome shown by the local people had dispelled any initial doubts that I may have had and I shall always treasure the time I spent in their midst.

# CHAPTER 4

# Seeing Red

Criticism is something we can avoid easily – by saying
nothing, doing nothing, and being nothing.

**Aristotle**

IN FEBRUARY 1993 I was selected to play for Wales B against
Holland in S'Hertongenbosch. The team met on the
Tuesday, prior to Saturday's match and we were able to have
two full days' practice together. Then we flew to Holland on
the Thursday, each player having been presented with a blazer
and grey flannels, the official dress code for the occasion. We
returned to Cardiff on the Sunday having had the luxury of
being able to concentrate on just the one rugby match for
almost a week. SWALEC had given me time off for that period
(without pay) and in that respect the company always treated
me well while I was an employee.

I was joined by two other North Walians in the B team, Stuart
Roy from Menai Bridge, who played in the second row for Cardiff
and who, like myself, was a former member of Menai Bridge
Rugby Club, and the prop, Ian Buckett, from Flint, who was
a fellow member of the Swansea front row. My father and Wil
Parry Williams, the Chairman of Menai Bridge Rugby Club, had
flown over especially to see my fist big game. It was particularly
nice to see them there and I always appreciated having family
and friends present on the occasion of important games. In that
respect my parents, my sisters, Naomi and Beth, and Tina my
wife were always been very supportive down through the years
during both club and international matches. Wil had always said
that he would be present when I played my first game for Wales

at senior level but he might have been a little disappointed that he wasn't able to fulfil that ambition somewhere in the Southern Hemisphere!

I would have liked to have been on the pitch for a longer period of time in Holland since my father and Wil had made such an effort to be there. Unfortunately towards the end of the first half I took a heavy blow to my head and had to leave the field. I knew, even before I was forced to go off, that things weren't right – I had apparently asked Paul Arnold, the Swansea second row, who our opponents were! In fact the same thing happened to me several times during my career and in that particular game against Holland, as on other occasions later on, I had to ask the line-jumpers to be patient with me for a while, and to tell me exactly where the ball was to be thrown, since, in my confused state, I wasn't able to decipher the code we were using! That kind of situation couldn't continue for long, of course, and in this particular instance I soon had to leave the field for good. Andrew Thomas, from Neath Rugby Club, who had a very good game, as we demolished the opposition 57–12, replaced me.

While I was on the field the Holland front row gave us no problem at all. However, it seemed that I was quite a disappointment to their hooker. For I had recently won a televised 'Strongest Man in Wales' competition on S4C (the Welsh Channel 4 Service) which was misleading as it was based more on fitness and endurance, a 'title' which has dogged me ever since! The hooker in question came up to me during the reception following the game, with a rather puzzled expression on his face, and said, "Strongest man in Wales? You're not the strongest man in Wales!" I don't know what he expected of me but it seems he'd been very worried before the game that he was going to have to play against *the* strongest man in Wales. This was one rare example perhaps of how the hype surrounding the S4C competition had worked in my favour and had somewhat undermined the confidence of the opposition before the game had started!

It did, however, provide plenty of 'ammunition' for team-mates to bring it up again (and again) in the future at my expense. For several years afterwards rugby coaches and fellow players would take some delight in trying to wind me up with such comments as *"Let's see how well the strongest Welshman can handle this next exercise!"* or *"We'll be alright against the Cardiff front row next week boys because we've got the strongest Welshman playing for us!"* The press never let me forget my 'title' either, for even up until the very end of my playing career in 2005 they still referred to me as "former 'Strongest Man in Wales'"!

One month after the Holland game I played for Wales A against Ireland at Pontypridd, on the eve of the match between the two senior teams in Cardiff. Ours was a particularly hard game, with David Humphreys, the Irish fly half, scoring 19 points as his side beat us 29–28. Although Alan Davies, the national coach, was particularly critical of the forwards, I was quite pleased with my own performance on the night and felt that I was able to hold my own in such company. In order to obtain a second opinion on how I had played I would always turn to my father. If he was happy with my performance – although it didn't always follow that he would be – then I was satisfied. Unfortunately, during that particular time, which was so different to the present professional era, there was a tendency to view the A team as a kind of pub side who would play their game on a Friday night, then stick together for the rest of the weekend in order to have a good time. Yet there was a good spirit amongst the lads and although many of them, such as Mike Voyle, Scott Gibbs, Rob Howley and Paul John, had played together since their schooldays I had no problem fitting in and was good friends with Ian Buckett and Paul Arnold.

By now I had settled in my new locality in Carmarthenshire.

The lads at work were just like the gang in the Llangefni yard, many of them being the sons of local farms and consequently very hard working. The nature of the work was a somewhat different than at Glyn Taff. Firstly there was a lot of travel time involved in getting to rural areas like Ystrad Aeron or Tregaron. Secondly it was much easier putting up poles on the streets of Rhondda than in remote fields in the countryside. But that kind of work seems to attract the same type of person and in that respect Llanfihangel-ar arth also had its fair share of 'characters', like Wyn 'Wombat' Davies, Clive Reynolds, Les 'Cochyn' ('Ginger'), Alan Davies and Bryan 'Ap' Davies. Perhaps the quietest member of the gang was one of the greatest rugby players ever to represent Llanelli, Wales and the Lions, the second row giant Delme Thomas. I didn't know much about him until my father mentioned that Delme was one of his own personal heroes. In our midst as a gang he was shy and unassuming and although we would chat occasionally about rugby in general it was very difficult to get him to talk about his exceptional achievements in the game.

At the end of the working day I would sometimes be very hard pressed to return to the yard and then get to Swansea Rugby Club in time for training. I would often be so pushed for time that I would have to go directly from work to St. Helens, but the usual drill was to drive to Carmarthen and then get a lift to Swansea with Alan 'Santa' Reynolds (he was the son of the Santa Clara Inn at St. Clears), one of the All Whites stars at the time. But the sessions at Swansea weren't enough for me and I still felt I needed to do some extra training on my own to enable me to improve on the required level of fitness, so at Capel Dewi I had to devise a new routine for additional fitness sessions. To that end I would go to a field behind the flat and go through my 'routines', one of them being the 'bleep' test.

In order to improve my aerobic fitness I would place a

tape recorder on the field and run continuously between two markers, keeping time to pre-recorded bleeps. This would allow me to measure how many runs I had done within a particular time. I would mark the distance (approx. 20 metres) I wished to run by putting my trainers on the ground, but often, when Tina was staying with me, her dog, Pepsi, would also come to the field and take great delight in running off with the trainers. As a result I would spend the remainder of the session running all over the field trying to catch Pepsi! It was quite an effective way of improving my fitness but should anyone have witnessed such an exercise at the time I shouldn't think he would have rated the 'sophisticated' training methods of certain top-class rugby players very highly!

In May of that year I was chosen to tour Zimbabwe and Namibia with the senior Wales squad, although the rugby pundits saw me as the second choice hooker to Andrew Lamerton. Nevertheless I'd won my place over Nigel Meek who'd played in the Five Nations Championship earlier that year. In fact I felt rather pleased with myself bearing in mind that I was one of only seven members of the squad who hadn't been capped by Wales and that Swansea had picked me for just six Heineken League games during that season. I'd really enjoyed representing my country at 'A' level, and wanted more of the same. However, for most of the tour I was a frustrated member of the squad.

The coach then was Alan Davies who was assisted by Gareth Jenkins, from Llanelli Rugby Club, who took charge of the forwards. We played three games in Zimbabwe, two of which were against the country's first team, and we won each one comfortably. I wasn't selected for any of them and neither was I given an explanation by the coaching staff as to why I was on the bench for all three matches. Perhaps I was at fault in that I didn't seek an explanation or guidance as to how I could perhaps raise my own game. But the situation had a very negative effect on my dealings with those in charge, which led to my adopting, in my own mind, an attitude of "Up yours!" which was always a fault of mine when dealing with people in authority. I remember Alan Davies, after the Zimbabwe games, noticing that something wasn't right and asked, *"What's wrong with you, Robin? You look as if you're ready to kill someone!"* I answered, *"Perhaps I am!"*

Nevertheless, Alan was a very pleasant person who got on well with everyone. I realise that I was still rather naive as a rugby tactician and perhaps lacking in perception but, at that time, I can't say that I was aware of any great vision that Alan and Gareth were able to convey to the players. Neither was I aware of any particular insight they might have had regarding what they were trying to achieve. I would have to admit, however, particularly in Gareth's case, that things soon changed in that respect.

The training sessions in those days were very much 'aerobic based'. Everybody began by jogging for a few miles then the backs and the forwards would separate to practice skills. The aim for us forwards was to get fit enough to enable us to reach as many rucks and mauls as we could during the eighty minutes. Methods are different now of course. The emphasis in the modern game is on being able to maintain mobility about the field, often in short, fierce bursts coupled with force. But of course adopting such a pattern means that forwards will not be able to get to every ruck and maul. Alan was quite a shrewd coach in his thinking, and would often introduce new techniques to his training sessions, and one example sticks in the mind of how he used his psychology. We were changed and ready to start training one morning whereupon he arrived and told us to stand in a circle, holding hands. Then he announced, *"Right! Now I want you all to sing 'Ring a Ring a Roses'."* We all looked at each other in amazement, but that was exactly what he wanted us to do, right up to the *"and we all fall down"* bit! At that point Alan announced that the session was over!

At last, however, I was selected to play, against Namibia B at Windhoek, which turned out to be a memorable occasion for me. Wearing the senior red jersey, for the first time in this particular instance, was a very special feeling, and remained so during the rest of my playing career. We won the game quite comfortably, 41–10, and I was quite happy with the way I played. However, the game stands out for me for two other reasons. Firstly I scored a try, after inter-passing with Neil Jenkins, and secondly I got sent off five minutes from the end! One of the Namibia players was tugging at my jersey as I ran for the ball so I swung my arm and aimed a slap, not a punch, in his direction. The referee saw things differently and I had to leave the field, although everybody who'd seen the incident thought that the ref had over-reacted. Robert Norster, the team manager, followed me to the changing room and said that we would be appealing against the decision. The appeal was successful and fortunately I didn't receive a match ban but that favourable decision made no difference, however, since I wasn't selected to play in the remaining two games on tour, against the senior Namibia team and the Barbarians, both of which were fairly easy victories for us.

Despite the frustration of having played in only one of the six games on that tour the social side of the trip was very enjoyable. In Zimbabwe, for example, we stayed at the luxurious Elephant Hills Hotel, which was an experience in itself. Wherever I have stayed in the world I have always wanted to take in as many different experiences as possible, so when we were given an opportunity to fly in a small four-seater aircraft over Angel Falls and along the Zambezi river, in order to see the amazing wild life there, I jumped at the chance! It was a fantastic trip. One to remember, too, for our flanker, Lyn Jones, the current Swansea-Neath Ospreys coach, as, once the plane had taken off, Lyn was petrified of looking out of the window. It was literally a white-knuckle ride for him as he gripped tightly the seat in front of him. That's the only time I ever saw him lost for words! To make things worse his suffering continued right up until the very end since the plane clipped a few tree branches beneath us as it touched down. We would have a chance to enjoy the local wildlife even as we trained on the golf course in the hotel grounds since there were many wild boars roaming there. Similarly baboons would surround us as we walked in nearby woodland.

Another factor, which could make a tour so enjoyable, was the contributions of the various 'characters' in the party. Players like Hugh Williams Jones, Tony Copsey and Rupert Moon. Lyn Jones was another and one who would take great delight in doing the unexpected. On this particular trip he had taken to drinking Earl Grey tea for breakfast. Nothing else would do and he had brought his own supply with him from Wales. He would also love to tease the lads and was able to do a great impersonation of Gareth Jenkins, which had the rest of us in stitches. But Gareth knew of Lyn's antics and enjoyed being part of the fun. One of his *fortes* as a leader was that he knew how to relax with the lads whilst he made sure that we, in turn, were aware that there was a distinct line, which wasn't to be crossed. One of his faults in some of the boys' opinion, however, was that he would insist that we, as a squad, sang the old Welsh favourites, like 'Calon Lân', 'Sosban Fach' etc. wherever we went. This would include the official receptions, which the British Embassy arranged on our behalf at various locations. Another character on the trip, but not for the usual reasons, was Mark Perego. He was a hard, extremely fit player whom you would like to have in your corner if you were ever up against it. He never touched alcohol and wasn't keen on the customary post-match socialising. He was different in many ways and would give the impression that there were many things that were so much more important in life than rugby, even when he was in his prime as a player. Wherever he went, even into the changing room, he would take this small porcelain pig with him, which he called Mr Peeg. On the plane from Zimbabwe to Namibia I remember him holding Mr Peeg against the window so that he could see the view!

Regardless of how much I had improved as a player I knew that I would spend most of the '93-'94 season at Swansea back on the bench, keeping company with other disappointed players in the squad, such as Mike Morgan, Dai Joseph and Ian Davies. Yet I enjoyed the training sessions, particularly under Trevor Cheeseman, and was happy with the way I performed there. I remember Mike Ruddock coming up to me at the end of one of the sessions to tell me that he was very impressed by my fitness levels. At that time the first team was again doing very well in the Heineken League and had been top of the table since the early part of the season. But I still felt the same frustration at not being asked to play in important matches. I was, however, picked in October to play for Wales A against the North of England at Pontypool and then against Canada at Cardiff in November. I was pleased with the way I played in that particular game and it seems that I made quite an impression on Clem Thomas, one of the stars of the 1950s when playing for Swansea, Wales and the British Lions and who was now a rugby journalist who wrote regularly for *The Observer*. *"I knew you were a good player before the Canada game, but I didn't know you were that good!"* was his remark to me at the Swansea club some two weeks later. I was aware that RCC Thomas was highly respected at St. Helens but I had to ask my father in order to appreciate the extent of his immense contribution to the world of rugby in the past. Therefore being complimented by Clem was praise indeed!

At the beginning of 1994 I was selected for the full Welsh squad for the Five Nations Championship although I didn't get to play in any of those particular games. Yet for about half a minute during the game against England I thought my moment of glory had arrived. Mark Perego got injured and I was told to take my tracksuit off in readiness as it looked as if I would be required to go on as a flanker. Mark, however, made a rapid recovery and I remained on the bench. That was the only game that Wales lost that season and we ended up as champions. I really enjoyed being part of the squad during the internationals, travelling with the team and participating in the post-match celebrations, which would always start with a dinner for the players and their partners in a plush hotel. By this time Tina took great pleasure in coming with me and socialising with the partners and wives of the other players. One notable change in my circumstances in those days was the need to acquire an appropriate suit, that is a D.J. with dicky bow, for those official post-match functions. Yet despite the air of sophistication that prevailed initially at these functions they often degenerated, by the end of the night, to the level of a normal Saturday night out with the lads. I remember the dinner, which followed that particular Twickenham game very well. Mike Catt had just been awarded his first cap and traditionally, on such an occasion, the player concerned would accept a drink from each of his fellow players, which he had to down in one, and he looked rather the worse for wear at the end of the night!

Team preparations for international matches in those days weren't nearly so thorough as they are today. It wasn't uncommon for Alan Davies to sit down with the lads the night before a game to discuss tactics over a glass of wine. We would meet up on the Thursday prior to the game and if we were playing away we would travel to the location in question on that day. We'd have a practice session on the Friday and play on the Saturday. On my first visit to Dublin with the team in February 1994, we walked to a local park, a short distance from the Westbury Hotel, where we were staying, to practice throwing in to the line-out, in front of members of the public who might have been in the area at the time. It was a great feeling to be part of the Wales set-up but if I had any grand thoughts that I had now 'arrived' as an international player these were well and truly quashed on the Friday afternoon whilst walking along O'Connell Street with two fellow members of the front row brotherhood, John Davies and Ricky Evans. A Welsh supporter rushed up to us and said, *"John, Ricky, good to see you, boys! Best o' luck tomorrow now!"* He then turned to me and asked *"Who the f\*\*\* are you then?"*

After the buzz of the Five Nations I had to think once again about returning to the Swansea bench, which made me quite depressed. A few months earlier Scott Gibbs had left Swansea and joined St. Helens Rugby League Club, and if one of the league clubs had approached me with an offer I think I would have accepted and gone North. The only escape from frustration for the reserve players at Swansea was to have as much fun as possible during the training sessions while the regulars in the team were being instructed in more serious matters. I can now appreciate that the attitude of some half a dozen fed-up players could easily have a detrimental effect on the general atmosphere in the squad and that is exactly what happened. Mike Ruddock blew his top and sent Mike Morgan and me to stand at the side of the field like a couple of naughty kids until 'we had come to our senses'. This perhaps was a rare example of players being given a yellow card during training.

But the situation did improve. Towards the end of that season Stuart Davies got injured and had to miss a few games, including the annual match against the Barbarians, and I was asked to assume the first team captaincy in his place. I'd done that job for the mid-week team a few times but it was quite a shock to be given that particular honour, by Mike Ruddock of all people, since we weren't getting along all that well at the time. However, I accepted and enjoyed the experience very much. I was never a captain who liked to make memorable, fiery speeches, neither before a match nor during half-time. I preferred to try and lead by example, from the front. I hoped that, if I were seen to be giving 110 per cent, that in itself would serve as sufficient inspiration for most of the team. In that respect Stuart Davies himself was an inspiration as he'd made a big impression on me during my time at Swansea.

The All Whites won the Heineken Championship that year and because I played in the final game of the season against Aberavon I was part of the victory celebrations. Yet in my particular case those celebrations had rather a hollow ring to them since I considered that my contribution to the club's success had been minimal. The Welsh selectors, however, still remembered me at the end of the season, for I was included in the squad for the two preliminary World Cup games in May, against Portugal and Spain (both of which were comfortable victories) and for a tour to Canada and the South Sea Islands in June, with Alan Davies again as Coach and Gareth Jenkins as his Assistant. We played five games in all on that tour, four of which were test matches against Canada, Fiji, Tonga and Western Samoa, which merited the award of full caps to the players. I was once again very pleased to be in the squad, bearing in mind that I'd played just six games for Swansea in the Heineken League that season. Indeed had Garin Jenkins not been suspended early in the season it's possible that I wouldn't have played a single game. Yet, on leaving Canada, where the team had two more comfortable victories, I'd been on the bench as a replacement for Garin on nine successive occasions. I'd begun to accept that perhaps I was never going to win my first cap. After all, poor Ian Buckett was on his third tour and was still waiting for that honour. Nevertheless I wasn't particularly keen to go and discuss the matter with the coaching staff.

But at last my big moment arrived in Fiji. In a fantastic hotel, overlooking a beautiful blue sea, golden sands and palm trees, in a gorgeous place called Nadi, it was announced that I was in the team to play Fiji in Suva, on Saturday, June 18, 1994, in place of Garin. I was really chuffed when I received congratulations from the rest of the squad, and later from Tina and my parents when I telephoned to tell them the news during the early hours in Wales. What amazed me was that such a large number of people in Wales had been so pleased by the news. That was evident from the very many congratulatory messages that reached me in Fiji, from friends, from Swansea Rugby Club and the clubs that I had played for in north Wales, from Mike Ruddock himself and from my employers at SWALEC. I've always appreciated receiving such messages but they were even more important on foreign tours.

We had to fly from Nadi to Suva in a very small, fragile-looking plane, on one of the most terrifying journeys we players had ever undertaken. Some of us had even begun to wonder whether we would make the match at all. Fiji were confident that they were going to win and they'd flown eight players back from New Zealand especially for the game, as well as two former members of the All Blacks, Bernie Fraser and Brad Johnstone, to coach them. In the loosehead prop position they'd selected Ron Williams, who toured Wales with the All Blacks in 1989, and, at tighthead they had selected Joel Veitayaki, who weighed over 20 stone, the largest prop in that position that I'd ever played against. He later joined Dunvant Rugby Club for a period. We were prepared for a tough match but one aspect of our game had to be modified at a very late stage.

At that particular time the rules concerning the line-out had recently been changed to allow jumpers to be held in the air by fellow players at the top of their jump but they were not permitted to be lifted to that position. Because of this new rule we asked the officiating referee to come and look at one of our training sessions and give his interpretation. So, during that particular session I was required to throw the ball in to Phil Davies, who had to jump for it without any assistance from other players in the line. Then, on the next throw, he went for the ball while being held in the air in accordance with the new rule. However, as Phil soared to catch the ball on the second throw, the referee was of the opinion that his fellow players did more than just hold him at the top of his jump. *"There is no way that man is jumping that high"* was his verdict, so we had to be very careful of our line-out tactics for the Fiji game.

The game was played in the National Stadium before a crowd of 20,000, in hot weather but not unbearably so. We won 23–8 and I was quite happy with my performance, despite the powerful front row, which opposed us. I got quite a buzz early in the game when I floored Batimala, the Fiji hooker, with a thunderous tackle, which drew a lively round of applause from the crowd. Supporters in that part of the world really loved to see strong tackling and they showed their appreciation in a remarkable way, by letting out a squeaky high-pitched laugh, which, although it sounded strange at the beginning, was something we got quite used to by the final whistle.

I was presented with my first cap (the first of 37 but perhaps the one I treasure most) by Dai Rees, a WRU Committee member at the hotel after the game,. I heard later that my parents had listened to the game on the radio back home in Wales but they decided to put the champagne and the cake shaped like a rugby pitch, which their neighbours had brought, on hold for a little since they didn't feel like indulging themselves in that way at three o'clock in the morning! I didn't play again on that tour  since Garin was selected against Tonga, when we won 18–9, and again against Western Samoa, a game that the home team won 34–9. I was, of course, disappointed for I had a taste of playing at the highest level and knew that I wanted more. However, I was really pleased for Ian Buckett who had at last won his first cap against Tonga.

As expected, the game against Western Samoa was very difficult. After all, three years earlier, they'd beaten Wales 16–13 in Cardiff during the World Cup. This time the match was played on a hard, dusty pitch, which belonged to the local Chanel College at Apia, since the National Stadium was undergoing maintenance work. The Wales team had to assemble about an hour before kick-off in stifling heat with temperatures reaching 33°C in a sauna-like tent beside the pitch, which served as a changing room. As the team travelled back to the hotel in a mini bus there was some concern for Rupert Moon, who'd fainted due to dehydration and was hanging out of the door throwing up. Some of the other lads, too, felt rather shaky. As well as the unbearably hot weather the home team's tackling had been so fierce that Mike Rayer confessed afterwards that he felt like he'd been in a car crash.

Despite my disappointment that I only played in one game on that tour our visit to the South Sea Islands was an amazing experience. Alan and Gareth were both very popular for the way they led us during the tour and we players had a lot of fun in each other's company and got to know each other very well. For example, I had been quite critical, to my way of thinking, of Tony Copsey and Rupert Moon, two Englishmen who had chosen to play for Wales. Both were amusing characters, but for a long time I found it difficult coming to terms with the idea of someone who was not a native of a particular country wanting to play for that country's national team. Tony, after all, had a tattoo on one part of his anatomy displaying the words "Made in England"! (Maybe that was the reason why John Davies, Ricky Evans and I had our hair cut quite severely during the tour, leaving the shape of a dragon's tongue, the symbol of the Welsh Language Society, prominently exposed on the back of our heads!) But I got to know them quite well during those weeks and I particularly enjoyed sharing a room with Rupert for part of that time. Indeed, as a result of that experience, the family and I became firm friends with him, a friendship that has lasted to this day. One particular tie that binds us is the fact that Rupert is godfather to our eldest son, Billy.

The South Sea Islands often evoke an image of paradise for many people and that's especially true of me as a result of that tour, with many aspects having created particularly fond memories for me. The day after the Western Samoa game, we were invited by one of their players to spend the afternoon on his private beach. The sky was blue, the sea was warm and crystal clear, and the beach itself was fabulous, with local houses, perched on stilts, dotted around its perimeter.

The warmth of the South Sea Islanders made a great impression on me. They are particularly fond of singing and dancing as we discovered on many occasions. In Nadi, as we left our hotel to fly to Suva for the game against Fiji, all the staff gathered to bid their goodbye in the traditional manner, with a song. When we landed in Western Samoa a number of islanders were there to greet us in the same way. But my most colourful and memorable musical memory of the tour was the performance of the brass band, which entertained the crowd before the game against Tonga at Nuku'alofa, in the presence of the King of Tonga. Possibly my views have been coloured by my days as a trombone player but this particular band's talents were truly amazing. Members of the band arranged themselves in such a way as to correspond to the positions a rugby team would adopt at kick off, with eight 'forwards' on one side of the field, with the 'half backs' and the 'three quarters' outside in a line, each one holding a brass instrument. On the centre spot one of the band simulated a kick to start the play, the forwards made as if to catch 'the ball', then formed a maul. Next the imaginary ball was despatched by the instruments of the other players across the field until it was 'grounded', for a try, by the winger. All this while they played a particularly stirring piece of music to send the imaginary ball from one to another. Fantastic!

During the tour we stayed at several different hotels, such as the Dateline Hotel in Tonga and Aggie Gray's in Western Samoa and, when there was an opportunity to relax, some of the lads liked to laze about the hotel pool, while others of us were keen to experience more adventurous activities. Such activities seemed enticing, but they sometimes got us into trouble. For example, in Nadi a dozen or so of us had a chance to do some scuba diving off a famous coral reef. The sea was very quiet when the glass bottomed boat left the bay near the hotel, with just a crew of one, but as we approached our destination the sea started churning fiercely, with the result that Phil Davies refused to get off the boat. Having donned the appropriate equipment the rest of us dropped over the side and despite the fact that we had no previous experience of that kind of diving, we were quite confident and were keen to taste the experience.

Before long we were all over the place, being thrown in every direction by the waves, which were breaking wildly above our heads, as the boat drifted further and further away from us. Having realised that we were in difficulties, Phil Davies was shouting frantically at the boatman, who didn't have much English, to try and get closer to us so that we could get onto the reef. Our problem was that we weren't able to see the reef through the boiling sea but somehow Paul Arnold managed to get there and stand upright like a beacon to direct us to him. In the meantime Phil had brought the boat as close as possible to the reef and was standing in the boat to drag the shattered group, one by one, back on board. As a result we didn't get a chance to try scuba diving proper but we were so glad to have lived to tell the tale. Ian Buckett was so distressed by his seagoing experience that he had to have a cigarette immediately after returning to the boat. It was rather a pathetic sight watching him try to light that soggy fag with shaking fingers. On another occasion also I got into difficulties in Nadi, with Tony Copsey, when we decided to go on a catamaran trip, for the very first time, across the bay. The problem was that no one had told us how to turn the catamaran around, so that we could get back. So after sailing out to the open sea we were forced to jump over the side, turn the boat around and climb back on board, this time with the katamaran's nose pointing towards the shore!

I returned to Wales having had an extremely enjoyable trip and hoping that I'd get many similar opportunities in the future. In addition, in the company of so many talented players, I knew that I'd learned a lot about the game of rugby. Indeed, I remember being amazed, on many occasions during the tour, at some of the skills that they displayed on the field.

# CHAPTER 5

# Going Scarlet

*If you don't hear opportunity knocking, find another door.*

**Anon**

A FEW DAYS before going on that tour with Wales Tina and I had moved to live in Tumble, Upper Tumble to be exact, since being based in Capel Dewi was a little inconvenient. Tina was working in Neath, which meant that she had a long journey from Carmarthenshire each time she stayed with me, so we looked for a more central location, near to the M4. We were warmly welcomed to Tumble from day one, particularly by our immediate neighbours, Graham, Julie, Alan and Minnie, who have been very supportive to this day. We still live in the same house, now with our two sons Billy and Harry, and Mali, the dog, which is proof in itself of how happy we are there.

Rugby, of course, is an important part of village life and doubtless there are those who would question the wisdom of choosing such a location. In a place like Tumble, however, any opinion on rugby is usually the result of hours of debate amongst friends and family. I have to confess that this is why I like living in the area but maybe my take on the subject would be different if I'd been part of that particular rugby culture from my earliest days.

The focal point of all such discussion is of course Tumble Rugby Club and I would go there often at one time and enjoyed many a great, late night. Family responsibilities and other various duties no longer afford me many opportunities to socialise there these days. Nevertheless I go along to support Billy and Harry when they play for the junior teams and I've had the pleasure on more than one occasion of presenting trophies to some of these teams during their award ceremonies.

Some people doubted whether, by going to live in Tumble, I would be able to escape the daily pressure of the rugby world when I might prefer some peace and quiet. In their opinion I would almost certainly come across someone wanting to discuss the fortunes of the Wales or Scarlets teams when taking the dog for a walk or popping out to the local shop – something that is even more likely to happen now that I have become part of the national team-coaching set-up. In the early days of course people would wish to point out that Llanelli was a much better team than Swansea! Almost everyone in the village, as in so many of the surrounding areas, has his or her own particular opinion on various aspects of the game. It is so different when I visit Brynrefail, the village near Llanberis where my parents settled and where my mother still lives, and meet someone who wants to talk about rugby (although such people are comparatively few in that area). They would usually have based their views on what they'd read in the *Western Mail* or *Wales on Sunday*...

When I moved to Tumble some people thought that I was already preparing to leave Swansea for Llanelli Rugby Club. That wasn't true and I was perfectly happy to continue playing for the All Whites, believing that I wasn't far from achieving my great ambition in the game of winning a regular place in the Wales team. However, some six weeks after returning from the tour to the South Seas, before the beginning of the 1994-95 season, we were enjoying a family barbecue at home when Alan Lewis, the Llanelli coach at that time, suddenly appeared the other side of the garden wall to ask if I fancied playing for the Scarlets. He assured me that I would have a regular place in the first team and would definitely be in the side to face the touring Springboks that autumn. The Llanelli boys who'd been on the recent Wales tour with me were well aware of the fact that I was unhappy at Swansea. Since Alan was also a close friend of Kevin Bowring, the Wales A coach, it was therefore more than likely that he'd heard that I was unsettled at St. Helens. The main reason for the interest shown in me by Llanelli was that Andrew Lamerton, their first choice hooker, was suffering from an illness, likely to keep him out of the game for some time. In due course it was established that his kidneys weren't functioning properly causing him to suffer severe back pains. That evening I informed Alan that I would give the matter my consideration over the coming weeks.

Early that season Llanelli visited St. Helens and I was chosen to play against them. We lost 23–35 and I was back on the bench for the next game, having to accept that I was once again part of the same old pattern. I knew the Llanelli captain, Phil Davies, quite well and he invited me down to Stradey to watch the Scarlets playing against Pontypool. In the meantime Alan Lewis gave me a call to ask for my response to his offer some weeks previously, so I had some lengthy discussions with Tina and my father concerning the possibility of moving to the Llanelli Club. The result of all this was that I decided to leave St. Helens for Stradey Park at the end of September. I telephoned Anthony Clement, the Swansea captain, to inform him of my decision and it was obvious from his reaction that he'd been expecting such news for some time. He accepted that it was the only way forward for me if I was going to improve as a player. Indeed everyone I talked to felt the same way, including the Swansea supporters, judging from the warm reception they gave me when I returned to St. Helens with Llanelli a few weeks later. That is, everyone except Mike Ruddock, who wanted me to speak to Kevin Bowring about my Wales prospects before deciding whether or not to leave. But by now my decision was final, and I was looking forward to a new challenge and a fresh start with Llanelli rather than carrying on with the same routine at Swansea.

I settled quickly at Stradey Park, for I knew many of the lads very well, like Ricky Evans, Phil Davies, Tony Copsey, Rupert Moon, Neil Boobyer, Nigel Davies and Huw Williams-Jones. I also had a lot of respect for the coaching team, led by Alan Lewis, ably assisted by Phil, Richard Jones and Anthony Buchanan, with Peter Herbert responsible for fitness. Llanelli's open style of play (to be fair Swansea also adopted a similar style) was right up my street and I was more than happy with my early performances for the Scarlets. I hadn't realised, in fact, how much I really enjoyed playing rugby until I had a run of games for Llanelli. Part of the pleasure came from the satisfaction of just playing regularly; yet I still thought that I didn't have enough top-class rugby under my belt. Starring in the occasional game for Swansea hadn't been difficult since I was only called upon to play once every three weeks or so. I found that maintaining the standard required on a regular basis, week after week, was much harder, yet that was my aim.

Another young player had joined Llanelli at the same time as me and I got to know him well both on and off the field. His name was Chris Wyatt, a very talented player, and over the years we established an excellent understanding with regard to the lineout. But Chris, of course, was not just a good line jumper. He also excelled in open play, proving to be very mobile about the field, which was rather surprising given that he was a heavy cigarette smoker throughout his career, one of the few top-class players that indulged in this way. He tried to break the habit at one stage, and took to cigars instead, but it didn't last. Chris was quite a character and we had a lot of fun in each other's company, especially over a post-match pint or two. His pre-match tastes, however, didn't appeal to me. Before each game he would have to eat a tin of Heinz baked beans and sausage, which he would always carry with him wherever we went! We both started out together at Stradey Park so it was a very rewarding experience for us, towards the end of our careers, to be awarded special caps to acknowledge our respective fiftieth Heineken Cup appearances. Only the Irishman, Anthony Foley, had beaten us to that milestone.

The biggest test I had to face during my first few weeks as a Scarlets player was the game against South Africa in November. As usual they had a very strong pack but I was quite happy with the way we dealt with their powerful front row despite the fact that we lost 12–30. The visitors came under a lot of criticism for their uncompromising rucking methods in the fierce tradition of Southern Hemisphere countries, especially since Wayne Proctor was badly injured as a result. I, however, have never been critical of those methods for I recognise the right of those countries to play a fast-flowing game, which is often hindered by defending players killing the ball by lying on it. I firmly believe that if a player lies on the floor and on the wrong side of a ruck, the opposition have the right to use their feet to remove him, on condition that the ball is within their reach and that they don't come into contact with a player's head. I have never deliberately killed the ball on the ground but I've often found myself on the wrong side of a ruck. Whenever I would be unable to move away quickly enough I would have to accept that my opponents' studs would unmercifully rake me, which was often the case.

During October I was back on the bench for the Wales matches against Romania and Italy in the World Cup preliminary rounds. So, too, in November against South Africa but this time I got to take the field for some fifteen minutes while Garin received treatment. They were a big physical team, with Uli Schmidt playing hooker, but I enjoyed the experience very much. I must have done fairly well, since Jeff Young, the former Wales hooker, described my efforts as being one of the most notable performances for Wales by a sub in such a short period. Praise indeed from an illustrious member of the front row union. As usual I had my doubts concerning the merits of the press reports on my performance. The only analysis I trusted was the one by my father, which he gave after every game, since I knew it would be honest and forthright. Throughout my career my parents would travel all the way from Anglesey to see me play home games and I would usually meet them for a chat some twenty minutes before the match. They would return home straight after the game and I would give my father a call late that night to receive the 'official' verdict on my performance.

In 1995 I was on the bench for Wales during the Five Nations Championship in Paris, Edinburgh and Cardiff and although I still enjoyed being part of the national team set-up at the highest level, it was a very disappointing season, with Wales propping up the table having lost every game. As a result the two coaches, Alan Davies and Gareth Jenkins, were sacked, along with the manager, Robert Norster. Such a response rather surprised me since we were champions the previous season and the World Cup in South Africa was almost upon us. Nevertheless I was still enjoying my rugby with Llanelli very much, despite the fact that our season had been rather mediocre.

Alex Evans, the Australian who coached the Cardiff team, was appointed national team coach for the World Cup, with Mike Ruddock and Dennis John as his assistants. Although I received some praise from Alex during the training sessions held in preparation for South Africa, it was a bit of a blow to be told by him as we left the training pitch one day that I wouldn't be included in the squad going to the World Cup. I was one of six Llanelli players who were part of the national squad earlier in the season overlooked for South Africa. The close relationship that Alex Evans enjoyed with the Cardiff players was evident from the squad he selected. Indeed, judging from the comments of some of the lads who made the trip there was an obvious division between Alex Evans and the Cardiff contingent on the one hand and the rest of the party on the other, even during social activities. My place in the squad was taken by Jonathan Humphreys, who was originally selected as a reserve for Garin but who became the first choice hooker in two of the three first-round matches in the competition. In those games Wales easily defeated Japan but lost to New Zealand and Ireland and the squad returned home immediately afterwards, having given a disappointing performance out there. Looking back to the period prior to the selection of the squad I remember being surprised at how often Jonathan Humphreys would ask Alex Evans questions about one thing and another. I realised afterwards that in those particular sessions I perhaps hadn't shown enough desire to know more, giving the impression to the coaches that I wasn't bothered. Jonathan's attitude certainly worked in his favour.

The fact that I had been overlooked for the World Cup during the summer, having been Garin's understudy for such a long time, made me realise that I would no longer be part of the Wales team set-up at the start of the new season. Therefore, I decided to concentrate on my career with Llanelli rather than be a fringe member of the national squad. Perhaps because I was enjoying my rugby so much at Stradey the decision didn't get me down.

Apart from the satisfaction I got from playing regularly, we had a lot of laughs and since 'winding each other up' was so prevalent amongst the lads at SWALEC I was easily drawn into that kind of environment and took every opportunity when it presented itself.

I didn't often have the opportunity to tease the lads in print but I did get the chance on the occasion of the final of the SWALEC Cup against Ebbw Vale at Bristol in 1998. I was asked to provide pen pictures of the Scarlets players for the official programme. So I decided to make the most of it. Here are some examples:

RUPERT MOON – This limp-wristed scrum half is often taken for granted and overlooked, rather than being heaped with praise. With a strut that would have made the late John Wayne jealous he is often the target and victim of foul play – although he needs no coaxing to collapse in a motionless heap.

WAYNE PROCTOR – Wayne is the image of pop star Paul Weller and is nicknamed 'the walking vein' because of his toned appearance. A world-class athlete whose dedication never wavers, he is a lethal weapon who can score from anywhere on the field. He is allegedly transparent when held up to the light.

CHRIS WYATT – Known as the 'One man riot'.....there is no questioning his ability and is acknowledged as one of the foremost sevens specialists in Wales. He has great footballing skills and is a superb, natural athlete who surprisingly maintains his high standards on a diet of milkshakes, pasties and menthols.

NEIL BOOBYER – Neil 'Baywatch Babe Boobs' typifies Llanelli's attitude of never being afraid to try anything. This sun seeking gambler loves to run at the opposition, but he is also more than capable of coupling that dash with some heavy duty midfield tackling. Deserving of his Five Nations cap this season, he is a keen amateur body builder who won't be seen dead in anything that doesn't carry a designer label.

As you can imagine I got a lot of stick from my fellow players, not just on the day, but also for some time after. But, I hear you asking, what was written to describe me?

Robin McBryde – Known to his team mates as captain chaos due to his infamous and sometimes explicit team talks,' was all that managed to find its way into the programme and I have my suspicions that Rupert Moon was the author of those particular pearls of wisdom.

At times the nature of my job also gave me ample opportunity to play a few tricks on my team-mates. Iwan Jones's house was wrapped from top to bottom in yellow polythene strips that we used to warn the public of electricity cables underground, including the chimney and everything in the garden. When his wife, Manon, came home with their daughters that day her initial thoughts were that it was a 'serious crime' scene and couldn't enter the house or garden. As it happened I'd already had a trial run for the exercise on Ricky Evans's house in Aberporth a few weeks previously.

You also have to keep on your guard so that you don't end up being the victim, and Dwayne Peel and Scott Quinnell almost succeeded in making me look a complete fool. They stole a life-size cardboard cut-out of me from the Welsh changing room - that are there for the benefit of visitors to the Millennium Stadium in Cardiff, and took it back to Tumble in their car. Knowing full well that the family and I had gone to stay at our caravan in Port Eynon, their intention was to leave the cut-out on the front lawn for all the world to see, giving the impression that I was the idiot who'd put it there. As luck would have it Tina had called at the house from work to pick something up en route to the Gower and happened to look out of the window when those two jokers were in the process of planting 'Robin McBryde' in front of the house! They had quite a shock when Tina suddenly appeared and had some trouble explaining their actions!

Leg-pulling and playing tricks were, and still are, part and parcel of the camaraderie that exists in being a part of any rugby team. One of the most recent examples being the 'feud' between Dwayne Peel and Mark Jones during our stay in France in the World Cup. After finding all the hotel's courtesy bicycles in his room, Mark singled out Dwayne as the main culprit. In retaliation he rounded up one of the sheep that roamed the hotel grounds and locked it in Dwayne's room. Dwayne returned to his room and couldn't believe his eyes, or the deposits that had been left everywhere! Knowing Dwayne, he's probably already got something lined up for Mark in the future.

I was really looking forward to the start of the 1995-96 season, with Gareth Jenkins now back at Stradey as coach. I'd been concentrating a lot on fitness during the pre-season period, and had enjoyed the official sessions taken by Peter Herbert. In addition, Craig Quinnell and I would often go to the club fitness room to do some extra weight-lifting. But we were now faced with a new development which was unfamiliar to us all, namely that the game was going professional. I remember Phil Davies holding a meeting at his home for the international players in the club in order to gauge our response to the proposal made by Kerry Packer, the Australian who shook the cricket world some years previously, to create a rugby 'circus' by signing up rugby's leading players to play all over the world, and be paid for it. Nothing came of the idea but the lads were quite taken by the idea. My main concern was to know who would be responsible for coaching the travelling teams. One thing was certain, if Mike Ruddock was going to be one of the coaches I didn't fancy going to the other side of the world to sit on a bench!

At that time the thought of giving up my job with SWALEC had never entered my head. I had, by now, moved to work from the Llanfihangel depot to Pontardulais, which geographically was much more convenient for me. Once more, as in the Rhondda, the café was a focal point in the daily existence of the gang. In due course that particular depot was closed and we all had to move to Clydach. Interestingly, the lads at work were divided on the matter of their rugby loyalties between Llanelli and Swansea and as you can imagine I would be given a lot of stick. On occasions the rivalry went beyond verbal discussion as we availed ourselves of every opportunity during our lunch break to take a football or rugby ball to the nearest patch of land. They were a great bunch of lads and I'm still in touch with some of them, like John Jones, Jason Bray, Richard Davies, Nigel Coppin and Mike Clement, the brother of Anthony Clement, who was himself on Llanelli's books at one time.

I had to be at my best at the beginning of the 1995-96 season since Andrew Lamerton had now recovered and was hoping to regain his place as the first-choice hooker. Gareth Jenkins thought a lot of him and I had to perform to the best of my ability to ensure that I wouldn't once again be spending my time on the substitutes' bench. I managed to hold down my place and believed that my own game had improved immensely since I'd become a regular member of the Llanelli front row. Playing constantly alongside the likes of Phil Davies, Spencer John, Ricky Evans and Huw Williams Jones had been a huge boost to my confidence and consequently to my performances. But the team had mixed fortunes in the league at the beginning of the season. We also lost to Fiji at Stradey and I was playing too when they defeated Wales A.

I had a small contribution to make to another international occasion at Stradey that autumn when I took the field for some 20 minutes in Ieuan Evans's benefit game. Stars from all over the world took part including Jonah Lomu, Sean Fitzpatrick, Rudi Straeuli, Kenny Logan, the Hastings brothers, Thierry Lacroix, Olivier Roumat, Jason Little, John Gallagher and a number of Wales players. Nineteen tries were scored in all, which meant that the crowd went home completely satisfied following a feast of open rugby. Yet I can't say that I enjoyed the occasion all that much. I never succeeded in tailoring my personal style of playing rugby to meet the requirements of benefit matches. I have never been able to give less than one hundred per cent on the field, regardless of the type of game I was playing in and the magnanimous, generous, rather light-hearted approach that was so typical of benefit matches didn't appeal to me at all.

I recall one such game when I was playing for Swansea against a guest team that included Mike Ruddock. At one point in the game I was haring for the line with a man outside me and only Mike in front of me. The custom in such a situation, in accordance with the spirit of benefit games, would be to pass to the player who was free outside me, and that was the signal I got from Mike as he closed in on me. However I thought that it was too good an opportunity to miss and decided I was going to run through him and put him flat on his back before crossing for a try. In retrospect I realise that I shouldn't have done that because a) he was my coach, and b) I didn't succeed in scoring!

Kevin Bowring became the Wales coach during the autumn of 1995-96 and I didn't think that my chances of being selected for the national team would be any greater under him than they'd been during the periods when Alan Davies and Alex Evans were in charge. Nevertheless I was in the squad for the Five Nations Championship but, once again, I was despatched to the A Team. Yet there was one slight difference. I was made captain for the first game against Scotland in Swansea. I imagine many would see this as a great honour but at the time it didn't mean all that much to me, for two reasons. Firstly I was quite bitter that I hadn't been given a second chance to represent Wales, despite the fact that, according to the critics and in my own opinion, I was playing consistently well for Llanelli week after week. I admit, nevertheless, that in harbouring such a grudge I was being rather immature.

There was perhaps greater justification for my second reason. I continued to feel that the A Team wasn't getting the respect or recognition that it deserved from the Welsh rugby authorities. They tended to think that little preparation was required before such a match and that, no matter what kind of performance we gave; the important factor was that we enjoyed a few pints together during the weekend. We lost that game against Scotland 22–31, and also against Ireland 11–25. During that second match our lineouts were a mess and we got hardly any possession from that particular aspect of the play. Mike Voyle was in the second row and fairly inexperienced at that time. Opposing him was Neil Francis, a wily old bird who succeeded, without being spotted by the referee, in spoiling every one of Mike's jumps. In such a situation Mike would have been justified in giving Francis a good shove or thump but he didn't have the guts to take it upon himself to do so. That occasion must have caused him some grief since he raised the matter with me again some years later after he'd joined the Scarlets.

Apparently the Irish A Team players received £850 each for that particular game while our reward was a meagre £30 each. In my post-match address, as captain, I remarked, with tongue -in-cheek, that the Wales A players must have received £10 for each lineout that we'd won! We were heavily criticised for our performance and for the lineout deficiencies in particular. Yet I didn't think that I personally should be taking all the flak for our weaknesses, so in my comments to the press and the media following the game not only was I very critical of the standard of our play but also of the indifference of the authorities, noting that perhaps the attitude of the officials towards the team sometimes rubbed off on the players. I was probably too outspoken in that respect and for the next game, against France, not only had I been stripped of the captaincy but I was back on the bench. I took it for granted that I had lost my place in the team because of the problems in the lineout, but it could also have been for my remarks following the game – which weren't supported by anyone else.

But before that game a new chapter in my life had begun, which was much more important than rugby. Tina and I had got married, in Gretna Green, so losing my place in the A Team shortly afterwards wasn't much of a disappointment. We'd got engaged in 1995 and had gone to Greece to celebrate. It was a very memorable holiday for many reasons, not least perhaps because it was our first foreign holiday together, and the last – so far! Since that holiday, the demands of rugby have always prevented me from holidaying abroad, while school term constraints have been a stumbling block for Tina, as she is a reception-class teacher. During our trip to Greece we became friends with Dave and Shirley Locke of Berwick Upon Tweed, and our friendship has lasted to this day. During our flight home we read on the back of the piece of paper on which they'd written their address the message "Don't forget we are only 50 minutes from Gretna Green!"

The more Tina and I thought about this the more we fancied the idea of getting married in Gretna with the minimum of fuss. So we started to plan for the end of February, and booked the Registrar, the civil ceremony and a local hotel for the wedding night without telling a soul, except David and Shirley, until the day before we travelled to Scotland. That's when we told our parents, firstly, in my mother's case, in the form of an apology, since she had always said, *"I don't mind where you get married as long as I'm there"*. The reaction of Tina's mother when she heard of our plans was, *"I wish you hadn't told me because now I'll be longing to be with you at three o'clock on Tuesday"*. When we realised the extent of their disappointment we regretted that we hadn't kept it a secret until after we'd returned home following the wedding.

To get to Gretna we flew to Edinburgh and drove from the airport to Berwick Upon Tweed to spend the night with David and Shirley. Then the four of us went by car through heavy snow to Gretna where they acted as our witnesses during the ceremony. The following morning Tina and I drove back to Edinburgh and flew home. On the way I phoned Anthony Buchanan, the Scarlets manager, to say, *"Sorry Buccs, I can't make training tonight. I'm on my way home from Gretna Green. Tina and I got married there yesterday."* And that's how the news was made public.

A few weeks later Tina and I invited some 300 friends and family to a memorable party at the Stradey Park Hotel so that everyone who hadn't been asked to the wedding could forgive us! We of course invited Dave and Shirley but on the morning of the party we got a call from them apologising that work commitments prevented them from being present. That night, as Tina and I stood in the foyer of the Stradey Park Hotel to welcome our guests, who should walk in but Dave and Shirley. The telephone call apologising for their absence had been made in Swansea and they had driven through the night from Berwick to get there! Their effort certainly gave the occasion a great boost.

As much as I tried not to show it, losing my place in the A team must have had an effect on my confidence and I naturally began to doubt and question my own ability. At Llanelli, Paul Jones, one of the jumpers, was constantly complaining that the throwing in wasn't to his liking and my response was to accuse him of not doing his job correctly. Indeed our bickering over the matter on the field led to us being warned by Gareth Jenkins to sort things out because the problem was affecting the general team spirit. It left me with two options, to ignore the problems, make excuses and deny responsibility, or face up to them and work to resolve the issue myself. So I made a decision to ensure nobody would have any reason to point a finger at me in future with regard to that particular aspect of the game. (I should have realised then that the hooker always gets the blame – whatever!)

In view of these difficulties I sought the assistance of Tony Waters, the Llanelli Club statistician, in order to analyse my technique when throwing in to the line, so that I could try to improve matters. As a result of that particular exercise I decided to change my technique. From then on I used two hands, rather than one, when holding the ball to throw in which is the method most first-class hookers now use. There are exceptions: Ibanez, the French hooker, being one who is able to master the direction of the throw using just one hand. Making such a change certainly seemed to work for me, and I took particular pleasure from the fact that I did it off my own back.

The Scarlets' mixed season came to a close with my being sent off by Derek Bevan, the referee of our game against Bridgend. He thought that I had used my boot in a dangerous manner on Steve Ford as he lay in a ruck. In my opinion I was aiming for the ball, not for Steve, and the video evidence, in addition to a letter which Steve kindly wrote in my defence, persuaded the WRU Disciplinary Committee that I was innocent. Although we finished in fourth place in the Heineken League in 1996 the fact that we would, as a result, be competing in Europe the following season gave us a lot of pleasure. In addition I was very satisfied with the way that I myself had been playing.

I remember Denley Isaac giving me invaluable advice when I was playing for Mold – advice I unfortunately didn't heed – that I should write notes on the hooker that I had just opposed at the end of each game. This would enable me to identify the strengths and weaknesses of his game ready for the next time I played against him. In the early days I regretted not having followed his advice but by this time I had got to know the characteristics of most of the hookers playing at the highest level and I'd learned which of them, for example, didn't like having their heads pulled down low, or didn't like having the opposing hooker use his head to drive in to their chest. It was important to bear all of this in mind before a particular match so that I could do those very things as required!

At the end of that season the Wales squad to tour Australia in the summer of 1996 was announced and, as expected perhaps, I wasn't part of it. Jonathan Humphreys and Garin Jenkins were the two hookers at the start of the tour but even when Garin was forced to return home through injury and Barry Williams was selected to take his place, I didn't mind at all. Being part of the Wales squad solely to sit on the bench had made me very unhappy for a long time and I'd come to the conclusion that this was now having an effect on me as a person. So, for that summer, I was happy enough to concentrate on my fitness under the supervision of Peter Herbert, paying particular attention to sprinting on the running track in Carmarthen.

# CHAPTER 6

# A Hooker's Lot

It is not the critic that counts, not the man who points out where the strong man stumbles or where the doer of deeds could have done them better. The credit belongs to the man who is actually in the arena, whose face is marred by dust and sweat and comes up short again and again because there is no effort without error and shortcomings, who knows the great devotion, who spends himself in a worthy cause, who at best knows in the end the high achievement of triumph and who at worst, if he fails while daring greatly, knows his place shall never be with those timid and cold souls who know neither victory nor defeat.

**Theodore Roosevelt**

IN RECENT YEARS there has been a considerable increase in the pressure to which the hooker is subjected during a game. He is, by now, one of the few players on whom the attention of the whole crowd is focused, as he prepares to throw in to the lineout. The team kicker is under the same kind of pressure. The hooker is no longer subject to the same scrutiny with regard to the scrum, since referees no longer insist on the scrum-half putting the ball in completely straight. Towards the latter part of my career, the hooker of the team putting the ball into the scrum would often not bother to compete for it. Instead his pack might concentrate on trying to shove their opponents backwards off the ball, pushing forward together the instant the ball is put in by the scrum-half. To see a scrum being taken against the head is a rare occurrence these days and that change has resulted in one form of pressure being removed from the hooker. However the opposite has occurred in the case of the lineout.

When I began playing first-class rugby no member of the pack was allowed to lift his jumper in the lineouts. As a result it was not all that easy to guarantee possession from that particular aspect of play and consequently it was not uncommon to see teams losing a lineout or two on their own ball. These days, of course, lifting jumpers is an essential part of the game and the team throwing in is expected almost automatically to gain possession as a result. Since the hooker, when preparing to throw in, has such an array of options open to him with regard to where he can direct the ball, in theory it should be too difficult for the opposing jumpers to work out where exactly it will go. Therefore if the forwards fail to win lineout ball on their own throw it is the hooker who is usually the target of the crowd's wrath. It is he who usually gets the blame if the ball flies over the head of the player jumping for it or if the opposing team's jumper grabs it before it reaches his own man. It is he who is usually deemed at fault if the ball falls to one of his forwards who was clearly not expecting it or if it lands in a gap with no member of his pack anywhere near it. As a former hooker and now a forwards coach I would like to illustrate, in defence of the players who still have to carry that particular cross, how complicated the whole process of the lineout can be.

Usually, a set of lineout calls would be agreed at the start of each new season. They would include a variation or two on the previous season's calls or sometimes a completely new set would be adopted. When I first played for Swansea, at a time when lifting lineout jumpers was not allowed, we would use a code such as *pink, yellow, mustard* when we had three jumpers in our line. If we happened to have five jumpers then we would have needed five words - one for each option. If, during the lineout, a word was called out which began with any letter in the word *pink* this signified that the ball was to be thrown to the front of the line; if the word called began with any letter in the word *yellow* the ball would then go to the jumper in the middle of the line. Similarly the ball would be thrown to the back of the line if the word called began with any letter in the word *mustard*. There are many variations, using the same basic principle, e.g. *Thames – Rowing – Club* or even *Front-Middle-Back!* There were possible additions to the call. For example, after any one of the 'code' words had been called, if the jumper in that particular part of the lineout secretly showed the palm of his hand to the hooker before he threw in, it would indicate that he was going to step forward to take the ball. If he showed the back of his hand then he was going to step back to take the ball. If the jumper clenched his fist that meant the ball was to be thrown directly to him.

Sometimes it would be the hooker's responsibility to give the appropriate signal. If he stood with the ball in his right hand, before throwing in, then the ball would go to a pre-determined part of the lineout. If he held the ball in his left hand it would go to a different spot and to a different place again if the hooker held the ball in both hands before throwing in. He might scratch his nose, wipe his hands on his shirt or run his fingers through his hair, (if he has any), and all with some sort of relevance to the calling system. In addition, the hooker would call out a series of completely meaningless numbers or letters before throwing in with a view to confusing the opposition even more.

All of this may sound complicated to some people but those particular systems were far less intricate than some of the codes used in the modern game, as the success of the lineouts back then would be based mainly on the understanding between two players, namely the hooker and his target. These days' lineouts have progressed even further, where the term 'pod' is used for the unit of three forwards that are used to win the ball. There are now more options available, with more players involved, and all with equally important roles to play. This means that the calling system needs to be straight forward enough for your own team to understand, but without making it too obvious to the opposition. One way of doing it might be with numbers,

*Who would have thought it*
*– Wales's Strongest Man!*

*With my sisters, Naomi and Beth.*

*Mr and Mrs Strong!*

*Bangor youth team. Sitting second from the left, Irfon Williams,
and second from the right, Alan Owen.*

*Porthaethwy youth team, with Chairman Wil Parry Williams on the left,
and coach Meic Griffith on the right.*

*The Mold team that played against Cross Keys in the cup.*

*Mold coach Denley Isaac.*

*Wil Parry Williams, May 1999, at the official opening of Porthaethwy rugby club.*

*Stuart Roy, Meic Griffith and me – Meic coached both of us.*

*At the book launch with some old friends from my MANWEB days, with Chris (on my right) and Ellis; and Robin Jones holding up his copy.*

*Some of the boys that looked after me in the Rhondda, including Viv (2nd from left) and Howard – who's bouncing Stuart on his knee.*

*Showing off the results of a hard day's work with John Jones (far right), and Mike Clement (front).*

SWANSEA RUGBY FOOTBALL CLUB
SEASON 1990-91

PLAYED : 43   WON : 30   LOST : 13   DRAWN : 0
Points for : 998   Points Against : 634

Semi-Final W.R.U. Schweppes Challenge Cup. Winners Cwm Tawe 7's.

REAR ROW STANDING - LEFT to RIGHT.
Paul Dowdeswell; W.R.Blyth (Chairman Selectors); Colin Muxworthy
(Team Attendant); Alan Williams; Alan Reynolds; Ian Buckett; Tim
Michael; Bleddyn Taylor; Mark Wyatt; Paul Arnold; Robin Jones;
Richard Moriarty; Nicholas Davies; Richard Webster; Mike Morgan;
Robin McBryde; Ian Davies; Kevin Hopkins; Steve White; W.J.Davies
(Selector); Byron Mugford (Team Secretary).

SECOND ROW SEATED - LEFT to RIGHT.
Keith Colclough; Trevor Cheeseman (Assistant Coach); Lloyd Isaacs
R.J.Dobbs (Club Chairman); Robert Jones (Captain);
Alan Donovan (Coach); Stuart Davies; Anthony Clement; John Evans
(Team Attendant).

SEATED ON GROUND - LEFT to RIGHT.
Simon Davies; Mark Titley.

*My first year as a member of the Swansea squad 1990-91.*

*Above left: wearing the President's XV shirt after playing against the All Blacks.*
*Above right: Swansea Captain.*

*The team that won the Cwmtawe 7's tournament.*

*Cymru v Fiji, 1994 – my first cap.*

*The crew that almost drowned! On the trip to the South Sea Islands, 1994, after a lucky escape!*

*Wearing my Cap.*

*John, Ricky and me with our tongues!*

*Running out as captain of Llanelli on Stradey Park.*

*The big day in Gretna!*

*Captain of the Welsh 'A' team before facing Scotland at St Helen's, 1996.*

*Face down at Stradey Park against South Africa.*

*Spencer John, Huw Williams-Jones and me in a cup match against Glynneath.*

*My first squad as Llanelli captain at the beginning of the 1988 season.*

*Rupert Moon and me celebrating winning the cup against Ebbw Vale at Ashton Gate.*

*Harry having fun with the stool!*

*Billy playing with the cup!*

*The two of them in Mr Moon's arms at Stradey Park.*

*Billy and me happy after a victory on Sardis Road – 'The House of Pain'.*

*Billy's first experience of the changing room!*

where each number from 1 to 9, signify a particular option. For example, number 1 might mean that the jumper in the front of the line will jump forward to catch the ball as it is thrown in. Number 6 might indicate that the jumper in the middle of the line is going to take a backward step before jumping straight up to gather the ball. Calling number 8 would mean that the forward standing behind the jumper in the middle of the line is going to turn and lift the man behind him. Similarly there could be particular significance, to the numbers 2, 3, 4, 5, 7, and 9. But things aren't quite as simple as that. It isn't just a matter of calling number 1 or 6 or 8 before the lineout, or the opposing forwards would soon be able to work out where the throw was likely to go each time. So the relevant number would have to be concealed in a code of four figures perhaps. For example, whatever the option chosen for a particular lineout, it's possible that the crucial number would be the third figure in a series of four each time. That is, if the code 9382 were called the pack would know that option 8 had been selected for that lineout.

Sometimes a team might choose a 'magic number' to signify which option would be in use at a particular lineout. That is, a specific number, let's say 2, would be given in every series of numbers which would form the code. The relevant option for that lineout would then be the one, which followed the number 2 each time. For example, if the hooker called 36726 then option number 6 would be the choice for that lineout. Once again there might be additions to the code, for example calling a double number, let's say 66 or 88, at the end of the code would indicate that the forwards intended to peel around the back of that lineout. Attaching a letter to the numerical code would mean that the pack intended to group around the jumper once he had landed with the ball in his possession, and then drive forward together.

However, on top of all this you have to study the opposition, look at how they have formed against you, and identify where your best chance is of winning the ball. Even then, at the last minute, if you take too long to get the ball in, the opposing forwards might move to mark that very pod. That's one reason why the forwards of the team throwing in might arrive at the lineout together, in one line, and choose not to form pods until the very last moment. Sometimes the call has to be changed so that the ball is thrown to a pod which isn't being as well marked. All this, of course, slows down the process and often explains why hookers are seen to delay before throwing the ball in. The pod system has also brought another change. The hooker used to wait for the jumper to be lifted before throwing the ball to him. Nowadays, when pods are in operation, he has the option of throwing the ball to a particular spot before the jumper is raised, so that both man and ball arrive there at the same time ... hopefully!

You can appreciate, therefore, that the business of throwing in at the lineout can be very complicated and that the hooker perhaps deserves a little more sympathy when things go wrong. Sometimes plans go awry even on the training ground without the hooker having to deal with the added disruption of a crowd of many thousands or the pressure arising from the expectations of a nation or a region, as is the case on match days. And he relies completely on members of the pack knowing their roles inside out so that the picture never changes, and everything remains constant. What you don't want to see is a blank face, where one of your team-mates is clearly struggling to remember what he should be doing and where he should be doing it. When that happens, you just hope that he's either trying to double bluff the opposition, or that the penny drops in time!

Naturally, your opponents are constantly trying to decipher your lineout code during a game and sometimes they succeed. I remember Scott Johnston recalling the time when he was a member of the Wallabies coaching staff and served as the team water-carrier on the touchline at the start of the Lions Tour to Australia in 2001. He would follow the play up and down the field and wore a microphone so that messages could be conveyed between him and the other Australian coaches. But the mike was also able to pick up the Lions lineout calls and by linking those calls to television pictures at a later stage the Wallabies were able to crack the Lions lineout codes, which would have been an important contributing factor to their winning the series.

Yet some of the methods employed to confuse opponents at lineouts can be quite simple, especially if the country has its own language! In Wales, for example, it is possible to shout calls in a language which other non-Welsh teams are not able to understand: Welsh. Steve Hansen adopted a particular system during his period in charge, which meant that all the Wales forwards had to be able to count to ten in the Welsh language. It was quite entertaining to hear the rather strange Welsh accents that sometimes emanated from the lineout, for example Brent Cockbain shouting in his best Brisbane Welsh dialect, or Colin Charvis trying to get his tongue around 'chwech'!

Confidence, as always, has a major part to play. When things are going well it's not difficult to put the ball in the right spot at the right time in the lineout and things seem to work together almost rhythmically. When confidence is low – that's when things change for the worse! The ball feels like a beach ball and every member of the opponents' pack appears to be well over six feet tall and coiled to jump. So the psychological factor, too, is all-important in the case of the hooker, just as it is with regard to the place kicker, since both are under the microscope to a far greater extent than other members of the team.

In the scrum, of course, the hooker is subjected to a different kind of pressure ... namely physical pressure and I really took to that particular aspect of the game. I used to assume that my duty in the scrum was to go after the opposing hooker by bearing down on him, bending him or lifting him – anything that would disrupt the opposing pack within the laws of the game. This was an integral part of my game, ever since my days at Mold Rugby Club under the guidance of Denley and in partnership with such a powerful prop as Roger Bold. But it wasn't easy to achieve this against, for example, Garin Jenkins, since he was a strong scrummager. At Swansea he also had a very strong unit packing down behind him. On the other hand it wasn't difficult to get Steve Thompson, the Northampton and England hooker, if sufficient pressure was put on him, to capitulate and shoot upwards out of the scrum. Perhaps some would criticise me for using such tactics but all I would say is that, bearing in mind how much of a hell-hole the scrum can be, a little sympathy is called for...and imagination! In any case the other team is usually at it too!

It's always important to try and understand how lenient, or otherwise, the referee is going to be with regard to the scrum. From my experience referees usually have no idea concerning what goes on in the boiler house of the scrum. However, when problems occur the referees feel they have to penalise someone, without necessarily getting it right every time. These days' clubs are able to obtain a dossier on almost every top-class referee. In it are statistics concerning the offences he chose to penalise in previous games, which offences he tends to penalise and how often he does so. It's possible, therefore, to obtain some idea before the game of what the referee will be looking for. Some are quite fussy, of course, but the worst type of referee, in my book, is the one who doesn't talk to the players, who doesn't explain his requirements as the game goes on, so that the players might know exactly where they stand.

This is where a lack of knowledge of the English language can be a problem at times, and I was given the advice when

I went to play in France for the first time that the important thing to remember with regard to lineouts and scrums was that certain referees chose to ignore every law pertaining to those aspects of the game when they were in charge. Therefore, from the beginning, I sought to discover to what extent I would be allowed to transgress before the referee decided to penalise me. If, in due course, he gave a penalty against me I would try to make sure that I wasn't caught committing the same offence a second time. Some of the referees I played under were great of course, such as Derek Bevan and Clayton Thomas from Wales, and the English referees Chris White and Tony Spreadbury. It is important to remember, however, that referees, like players, have good and bad days and they would probably be the first to admit that.

# CHAPTER 7

# Winning Battles

If you think you are beaten, you are.
If you think you dare not, you don't.
If you like to win but think you can't,
It's almost certain that you won't.
Life's battles don't always go
To the stronger woman or man,
But sooner or later, those who win
Are those who think they can.

**Anon**

THE 1996-97 SEASON took us well and truly into the professional era. I was still employed as a linesman by SWALEC but some of the Llanelli boys were earning their living just by playing rugby. As far as fitness and playing standards were concerned I was determined that there would be no difference between me and any member of the team being paid to play full-time. I made quite an effort to train on my own as well as attending the evening sessions at Stradey. I was never one for arguing over financial matters and I had always considered myself lucky to have the opportunity to play rugby at the highest level and enjoy a pleasant lifestyle as a result. Yet when the time came for me to discuss my new contract with Stuart Gallagher, the Club Chairman, I felt that with regard to the financial terms being offered I was being penalised because I had employment elsewhere. However, it wasn't something I wanted to complain about and there were a number of developments which augured well at the start of that season. One of them was Gareth Jenkins's decision to make me Vice-Captain to Ieuan Evans, which I considered to be quite an honour.

We had a disappointing start to the season, losing to Bridgend and Neath. In that second match I played opposite Barry Williams, who was selected to play for Wales against France at the end of September. I always enjoyed playing against him simply because I usually succeeded in getting the better of him in the tight, but he would be very prominent in open play and always gave the impression on the field that he had a lot of confidence. This might have contributed to the Wales selectors' decision to go for him, rather than Jonathan Humphreys and Garin Jenkins. Indeed, in an interview with the rugby correspondent of a local newspaper in South Wales, Barry claimed that they were now the three hookers who would be battling for the hooker's position in the Wales team.

However, during September a large cloud descended over the family, which meant that rugby paled into insignificance. That summer my sister Naomi had graduated from York University and had decided to return home to Menai Bridge. Soon after doing so she began to complain of feeling unnaturally tired and went to see the family doctor. He prescribed a course of antibiotics but, a day or so later, she returned to the surgery with a rash. She was given a blood test and later that day the doctor came over to the house to tell her that she needed to go to the local hospital the following morning to have further tests. Once these were completed she was informed that she should go home to pack her bag before being immediately admitted as an in-patient for further tests.

The following morning, in the presence of my parents, she was told that she had acute myeloid leukaemia. She initially shed a few tears but soon decided that she was going to live to be 'an aunt', for Tina and I were expecting our first child. Initially she was informed that her treatment would begin within a few days but they found that the disease was rampant in her body. Within hours she had been given her first dose of chemotherapy.

My parents had contacted Tina immediately at work and she came straight home in order to be there by the time I arrived. I found it hard to take it all in when I heard the terrible news, and couldn't believe it. To me that kind of nightmare was something that happened to other families. We were all so close, since we only had each other, both my parents being only children. Tina and I left for north Wales at once and arrived at Ysbyty Gwynedd in time for evening visiting.

At the time, the family received very little information about the disease although we later found out that it could be a rapid killer. Yet, if the patient responded positively to treatment, the prospects were good. During that period my father was about to undertake a visit to Lesotho, in Africa, to establish links between his school, Ysgol Cae Top, and a school in that country, but the hospital specialist suggested that perhaps he should postpone his trip, which of course he did.

In case the different kinds of treatment available to Naomi, such as chemotherapy and stem cell transfer, were ineffective there was one other possible process, which could save her, namely a bone marrow transplant. With this in mind Beth, our younger sister, and I had to undergo tests and fortunately I was a perfect match. Naomi enjoyed teasing me afterwards that I almost passed out when I gave blood for that test but I, too, took pleasure in pulling her leg that she now depended on me and should therefore refrain from offending me!

Naomi was in and out of hospital for six months, with my mother also there for the first two months as moral support. She had an extremely positive attitude, even concerning the hair-loss that would ensue after 'chemo'. But before her first 'chemo' treatment, she had a visit from Linda, the daughter of Mrs Davies, the cook at my father's school. She was a hairdresser and came to the hospital to give Naomi quite a severe Grade 3 haircut, so that she would not have to suffer the trauma of losing her hair as a result of her treatment. Of course Naomi had her low periods but, with the remarkable support of the staff of Alaw Ward, under the very special guidance of Sister Manon and several doctors, in addition to the support of family and friends, she pulled through. Naomi, having spent many years living and working in County Durham, has now returned to Gwynedd with Tim, her husband, and their children, Gruff, who is five and Matilda, two. Beth is now living in Hitchin with her dog Ed.

Like the rest of the family I was badly shaken by Naomi's illness and the experience changed my attitude to life in general. It made me realise that I should aim for a greater sense of purpose in life, for myself and my family, rather than exist from day to day, being satisfied with short-lived pleasures. Not that I was used to taking life lightly or that I would ever hold back from putting one hundred per cent into whatever I did. But I realised, at that particular time, that I should take my future more seriously. Consequently, after Naomi's illness, I think I became more contemplative and spent more time turning things over in my mind. Some months later, when Billy, our first son, was born and following an unfortunate incident connected to that occasion, I had even more cause to reflect along those lines.

Naturally, at the outset of Naomi's illness, and before she began to respond to treatment, I had no desire to play rugby. Llanelli Rugby Club, and Gareth Jenkins in particular, were very considerate and told me to take as much time as I wanted away from the game and to make Naomi my priority. As the season progressed and as my sister began to get better I felt the urge to resume playing once again. A particular development that hastened my return was that Ieuan Evans, the Llanelli captain at the time, had to give up playing for a while because of injury. As a result, as vice-captain, I was asked to take on the captaincy, which proved to be a very rewarding and enjoyable experience. Yet, on reflection, the Llanelli squad was quite weak at the time, especially that we were now competing on the European stage.

However, we had one new star who became a great hero at Stradey, the outside half, Frano Botica, who had played for the All Blacks. He was the first overseas professional to sign for the Scarlets and he became an example and an inspiration to many at the club, particularly in the case of young players like Stephen Jones. Frano was a very popular character, with a completely professional attitude. Indeed he was the only kicker I saw ask Wayne James, who took care of the rugby balls at Stradey, to ensure that the air pressure of our match balls corresponded to a specific number of pounds to the square inch. And given Frano's prodigious success as a goal kicker it had obviously been worth his while going to such trouble.

He was the mainstay of our success against Leinster, the game that opened our European campaign that season. Later we also defeated Pau at home, in an explosive encounter that saw Iwan Jones being sent off. We lost our two away games to the Borders and Leicester, where Vernon Cooper played his first game for Llanelli, at the age of 19, and did exceptionally well against Martin Johnson. We got through to the next stage, and played away against Brive. It was a memorable game for many reasons, mainly perhaps because we lost and, as a result, were knocked out of the Heineken Championship for that year. But it was the environment to which we were exposed that stays in the mind.

The snow was thick on the ground when we arrived in Brive so the French Army were called in to clear the pitch to enable the match to be played. The atmosphere and the enthusiasm of the crowd were so different to that which we were used to and it was quite a revelation to see how fired-up club rugby can be in the south of France. After the game refreshments for officials and players weren't provided at the club, as is the custom in Britain, but in a specially erected pavilion nearby, which could accommodate a few hundred people. Supporters were invited to join with the players at the post-match reception, and it was an occasion the whole town seemed to take part in.

For me, and for the rest of the boys, I'm sure, playing in Europe had been the highlight of the season so far. We were all looking forward to, hopefully, finishing in the top four in the Welsh Club Championship at the end of the season so that we would have another bite at the Heineken Championship the following year.

But my greatest thrill during that particular period was the birth of our elder son, Billy, in October, at Glangwili Hospital, Carmarthen. I stayed with Tina to wait for the big moment but owing to some complications I had to leave the delivery room before the actual birth. Happily I didn't have to wait long before I was told that Billy had arrived. It was a tremendous feeling for both of us but Tina didn't know whether she'd given birth to a boy or a girl until quite a while later. She felt so weak after enduring an emergency Caesarean that she wasn't really aware of what was happening around her. But once she was fully awake she had hoped that the colour of the baby's shawl would tell her what she wanted to know ... that she'd had a boy if the baby was wrapped in blue or a girl if the shawl was coloured pink. Unfortunately the little one had been given a yellow shawl so some time went by before she knew the score!

Soon afterwards I played for the Scarlets against Swansea at St. Helens and after the game some of the team and a few other friends took me to a club nearby 'to wet the baby's head'. Apart from the fact that we were, perhaps, just a little noisy we weren't a problem for anybody. Nevertheless, the bouncers on the other hand had decided, without saying a word to our group, that they would show us who was in charge. One of them struck me on the head with a bar stool and another floored a friend of mine, Mark Rees, with a beer crate as he stood over me while I lay unconscious on the floor. When I came round I wasn't able to recognise Mark since he had so much blood on his face. He eventually had over fifty stitches.

As a consequence of the incident I came to realise how vulnerable professional players had become when out enjoying themselves, especially in a group. This is particularly true of places where alcohol is available and where you leave yourself open to those who like nothing better than causing trouble. That incident in Swansea underlined for me that I now had new responsibilities and that going out on the town no longer appealed to me.

I had initially lost my place to Barry Williams in the Wales 'A' team to play Scotland early in 1997. However, he had to withdraw because of illness and I was selected to take his place. We lost 11–50 and it was a new experience for me to be a member of a team that was booed off the field after a disastrous performance. Our coach was Mike Ruddock but the old indifferent attitude concerning 'A' team standards had not changed at all in my view and I began to feel that I had nothing to gain from playing for the Wales 'A' team in those days.

I preferred to concentrate on the efforts of Llanelli and as the season drew to a close we had plenty to fight for. We reached the semi-final of the SWALEC Cup and lost for the third time in succession. In the League we went from October until the final week without losing a game and in the end it was a battle between Pontypridd and us for first place. Unfortunately they became champions but it was no mean feat for us to come second considering that our squad was still missing some top quality players. Indeed the club was struggling financially by this time and at the end of the season a meeting was arranged between the players and the committee to see whether it would be possible to cut down on spending. Perhaps it was an indication that Llanelli had not quite come to terms with the new professional era that one of the committee members suggested that ceasing to supply sandwiches for the players at the end of training sessions would save the club some money! As a result of that meeting the players agreed to take a cut in their earnings the following season.

Also at the end of that season the Lions squad to tour South Africa later that summer was announced and Barry Williams was selected as one of the hookers. About the same time it was announced that he would be moving from Neath to play for Richmond on a fairly lucrative contract. Yes, big money had started to appear but none of it was flying my way! Wales had also arranged a tour that summer to Canada and the USA, where six games would be played, three of which were Test matches. The two hookers originally chosen were Jonathan Humphreys and myself, with Garin Jenkins, surprisingly perhaps, having been overlooked. However, owing to injury, Jonathan had to withdraw and Garin went in his place after all.

I didn't consider myself as understudy to Garin for the Test matches and I was therefore disappointed that he was given the hooker's berth for the first game against the USA in North Carolina. I must confess that I had a feeling of '*déjà vu*' when the team was announced. The Welsh performance was disappointing although we won 30–20. The second Test was in San Francisco and I was chosen to play. Once again it was a tight game and, with fifteen minutes remaining, the score was level at 23–23 all. We somehow scraped through 28–23 after a below par performance. I was back on the bench for the next Test against Canada in Toronto even though I thought that I had done enough in San Francisco to retain my place. I'd got the feeling, by this time, that, even if Garin were to break his leg, his chances of playing in the Test matches would still be 50–50!

As the team prepared for that last Test match, rather than stand about kicking my heels while Kevin Bowring rehearsed some moves with the players, I strolled over to the other end of the field to join the rest of the squad who were doing some fitness exercises, in the hope that I'd get rid of some of the frustration I was feeling. Kevin blew his top and asked me what on earth I was doing. We had quite a bust up during which I complained about how unhappy I was that no one had bothered to explain to me why I hadn't been chosen for that first Test or why I'd lost my place for the last test.

Even if nothing else came from that quarrel it certainly cleared the air. Kevin was a good coach who had a great understanding of the game and, in my opinion, Wales certainly lost out when he decided to join the England Rugby Academy. Yet I felt that I hadn't benefited at all from my dealings with him, which was also true of my relationship with Alan Davies. The main reason for this, I admit, was that my attitude towards them wasn't perhaps sufficiently mature to enable me to capitalise on their talents. I realise now, looking back, that I chose to blame others, instead of looking to improve my own game.

I do feel however, that players, especially those who are still developing, are more likely to gain confidence if they know exactly where they stand and if the coach shows enough confidence in them by selecting them to start, or to be on the bench, for a run of matches. This would ease the pressure on players who fear that they are going to be judged on perhaps one game only. For that very reason they might not do themselves justice nor play to they're full potential. No such scheme was being operated during my early days in the Welsh squad or I would probably have reacted differently. I realise the situation has changed dramatically since the law changes regarding the use of substitutes, a factor which now plays a big part in the coaches' tactical approach. But a coach's attitude, as with Steve Hansen and Scott Johnson, who were both prepared to sit down with players to explain and discuss matters, also makes a difference.

I was of the opinion that the tour to Canada and the USA was a mistake with regard to the way it had been arranged. Six of the best Wales players were, at that time, touring South Africa with the British Lions, so, instead of treating the trip to North America as all important and playing Test matches there which we were expected to win, the Welsh Rugby Union should have stated at the outset that it was going to be a development tour with the emphasis on experimentation. After all, neither Canada nor the USA were considered strong teams at the time and winning against them would not have been seen as a great achievement. As a result there was a feeling amongst the players that it was going to be a trip to enjoy as opposed to one that would require hard work. Maybe it was that attitude that led Arwel Thomas, Nathan Thomas and Gareth Thomas to colour their hair yellow during the early days of the tour, until Kevin Bowring noticed and ordered them to revert to their original colours.

When we returned home from the tour, Llanelli's financial situation was the subject of much discussion with the pessimists, predicting that it wouldn't be long before the club folded. I, however, was looking forward very much to the new season for it would be the pinnacle to my career so far. The reason for this was that Gareth Jenkins had made me captain for the 1997-98 season. He had always stressed, at every opportunity, that playing for the Scarlets was a great privilege. He would regularly remind the team that they were representing the hopes and aspirations of a town and a region that were so aware of the history, tradition and achievements of the club and that Llanelli was a name that was respected wherever rugby was played. For me to be made captain of a club with such status was a huge honour and I was determined to try and do my duties justice during the year ahead.

The highlight of the first few months was the big game

against the All Blacks at Stradey. So much had been said about the achievements of the two teams, particularly with regard to the famous Scarlets victory of 1974, that, in the days leading up to the match, the whole area was buzzing with anticipation and local expectations were running high. Ironically, as it turned out, that 1997 game proved to be Llanelli's darkest hour on many counts. We lost 81–3, the biggest score ever recorded against the Scarlets. Nevertheless, funnily enough, I didn't feel any shame as captain on the night. I knew that the boys had given their all but the All Blacks had played sensational rugby, which was almost impossible to defend against.

Gareth Jenkins's immediate reaction, when he came into the changing room after the game, was, *"Well, there wasn't much you could do about that!"* Our only solace was that it had been a close game for the first twenty minutes, then the floodgates opened and players like Christian Cullen and Jeff Wilson ran riot. If I had been asked afterwards how the battle in the tight had gone I would have answered, "What battle?", because, on their put-in, as soon as the two packs had engaged, the ball would be out and away in a flash. On our ball they would be perfectly happy for us to get possession, whereupon they would hunt us in numbers, knock us down and then take the ball from us! As a result of the vast difference that existed between the two teams I think that the New Zealand rugby authorities came to a decision, following that game, that the All Blacks would never again, during future tours, play against an individual club. The gulf between both teams was evident, and after a brief word of praise for the All Blacks in my after-match speech, and thanking them for the lesson they'd given us, I sat down without further ado!

I suppose it would be fair to say that we had a mixed season in the League in 1997-8 since, once again, our squad wasn't strong enough, particularly when we were struck by a spate of injuries. As a result, I had to play tight-head prop in a few games at the end of the season, against teams with renowned front rows, such as Pontypridd and Neath. I must confess, however, that I enjoyed the experience, since playing hooker and tight-head have much in common. The tight-head prop, for example, like the hooker, must have a strong right shoulder so that he can weigh down on the opposing loose head to prevent himself from being lifted. It was suggested, early in my career, that perhaps I might wish to play tight-head as opposed to hooker. Indeed it's not uncommon in France to see the tight-head and the hooker exchanging places. But in my view the hooker has other duties to perform about the field which makes his position a little more interesting.

We didn't succeed in getting through to the last eight in the Heineken Championship in 1998 but I remember that particular competition for one reason only, namely the barbaric way in which Pau played against us in France. We'd experienced some of their brutal methods the previous season but we hadn't anticipated such deterioration in their standards. They won 44–12 but all my efforts that afternoon were channelled into making sure that my players were unharmed by mainly having to resort to threatening behaviour towards the opposition, way after the ball had gone. I really was concerned about our safety on the field especially since the referee wasn't inclined to do anything to protect us. The Scarlets have always opted to 'play rugby' and I can't recall any occasion when we went out onto the field with the aim of hurting opposing players off the ball. Of course, we are able to defend ourselves as effectively as any team against teams who are set on causing trouble. But the ball was of secondary importance to Pau, and with regard to scoring points, they obviously preferred the methods of the boxing ring but without even respecting the rules of that particular discipline either.

Before the season came to a close I was very glad to accept an invitation from Mold Rugby Club to open their new synthetic rugby pitch. I always try to return to north Wales as often as possible in an attempt to promote rugby there and in order to ensure that I won't forget the kind of background I myself came from. Many different ways have been tried to raise standards there, and it is without doubt a difficult task. But I don't think that the best way forward is to have, as was the case up until last season, the best clubs in the north play each week against teams from south Wales in Division Three of the National League. This calls for a remarkable level of commitment from the players, which will, in time, I'm sure, be found wanting. Teams from the south also find it difficult to travel all the way to Llangefni, for example, even though it is only once a season. The answer, in my opinion, is to establish a semi-professional team in the north, which would include the best players from the clubs located there and some five or six players who wouldn't quite have made the grade at the highest levels in south Wales, but would be prepared to commit themselves to spending time with the new team. All the team members would receive fair payment for their services and, in due course, would play against the four regional sides in south Wales, in addition to other teams during each season. The professionals would at this stage, easily beat such a north Wales team. However, if the right commitment from the squad and suitable coaching by experienced staff would be forthcoming, I think such a scheme could work.

There would be other advantages. At present a number of players from north Wales join clubs in the south and, after failing to make the grade at the highest level, they disappear amongst the lesser clubs in the south. Establishing a respected semi-professional club in the north would perhaps be a means of keeping the best players in that part of the country. Between matches, apart from the periods when they would be working with the squad, say on tactics or analysis, the coaches of the new team and its group of quality players could spend time visiting individual clubs to promote the game in those areas. The club players who would be part of the squad could draw upon their experience with the semi-professional side to the benefit of their fellow players in the club teams. All of this would be an effective way of improving rugby standards in the north and could even prepare the ground for making it the Welsh Rugby Union's main development area. And who knows, we could see the north, one day becoming the Welsh Rugby Union's fifth regional team, which, perhaps, could compete for the Parker Pen Trophy!

Despite some disappointments along the way Llanelli finished the 1997-8 season in triumph by winning the Hyder (formerly SWALEC) Cup, and beating Ebbw Vale 19–12 in the Final at Ashton Gate in Bristol, with Martyn Madden hitting the headlines with a memorable try, followed by his quote of *'That's show business!'* It was a great feeling as a player and in particular as captain to have won this game, since in the preceding years, we'd lost in the semi-final three times in succession and that this was our first trophy since 1992-3. I had never been a full member of a team that had won a trophy before, apart from the Swansea team that won the Cwm Tawe 7s competition! It's true that I was part of the Swansea squad when they became Heineken League Champions in 1993 but I wasn't a regular member of that side and I felt that I had achieved something much more important at Ashton Gate. I also sensed that, after quite a difficult period, the tide was beginning to turn for Llanelli and that I was getting the chance to show my colours as a person, to express myself as a player and to use my influence, for the better, as captain.

I had little opportunity to make an impression at international level in 1998. At the beginning of that year I was on the bench for Wales A, the fourth choice hooker behind Barry Williams, Garin and Jonathan Humphreys. Then I was selected for Wales A against Ireland and France, with Barry Williams now becoming the fourth choice after having started the season in first place. I was glad of the opportunity to play for Wales A again, although my hopes of getting back into the first team squad weren't high. However, at the end of that season, following disappointing results against France and England, Kevin Bowring resigned as the Wales coach.

# CHAPTER 8

# Back in Favour

They always say time changes things, but you actually have
to change them yourself.

**Andy Warhol**

BEFORE THE BEGINNING of the 1998–99 season Graham
Henry became the Wales National Coach. His name
was new to me and I didn't expect to see any change in my
personal situation under his command. His first significant
contribution, that September, was to hold two trial matches,
one in Cardiff and the other in Swansea, in order to run the
rule over the leading players in Wales at the start of the season.
I was chosen as a replacement for the Swansea game but I
had no opportunity to have a word with Graham concerning
my personal aspirations nor about what part I might be asked
to play in his plans.

There was a positive, encouraging atmosphere in the Llanelli
club at the start of that season and a general feeling that the
uncertainty that had hovered like a dark cloud over Stradey for
the previous two years had now disappeared. Maybe this had a
bearing on my choice of music, as captain, to greet the Llanelli
team as we ran on to the field for our home games. I wanted
a song that would be an inspiration to the team, which would
also be catchy enough for the crowd to sing and which would
serve as a reminder of what we stood for. Not every player was
familiar with the song at the time and most of them couldn't
even understand the Welsh words, until I provided a translation.
It was a very popular song at the time, entitled 'Yma o Hyd '
(We're Still Here), and composed and recorded by the well-

known Welsh singer, Dafydd Iwan. Once it had been played on the team coach it was unanimously agreed that it should be 'our' song.

Just before the start of the season a training camp was arranged for the players in Pembrokeshire. The aim was to give them an opportunity to get to know each other, particularly those who had joined the club during the summer, players like Salesi Finau, the centre and winger from Tonga. On the field there wasn't a tougher or fiercer competitor and his wholesale commitment made him a great favourite with the Stradey fans for many years. As a team we depended heavily on him and Scott Quinnell to use their strength to cross the gain line and take out three or four of the opposing team. In contrast, off the field he was so pleasant and endearing. He was a teetotaller, would always pray before taking the field and regularly attended church on Sundays. Like so many players from that part of the world, Salesi was a very likeable character and it was a privilege to have played with him.

It was nice to get some good results under our belt early that season, which was my second as captain. The players were particularly pleased, since the club, for the first time, had offered us contracts that were performance related. In other words, we were played less if we lost. The players called a meeting to discuss the new scheme, since some were unhappy with it but, for my part, I considered it to be fair. Indeed, as the season developed, it turned out to be rather lucrative for us!

We did rather well again in the Heineken Cup Pool matches, with good wins at Stradey against Stade Français and Begles Bordeaux and an excellent victory, 34–27 ( despite being behind 0–21 at one stage), away to Leinster, who were coached by Mike Ruddock. I remember two things in particular about that game. Firstly we had three Boobyer brothers playing for us that day and they each scored a try ... a record perhaps? Secondly, I went through the game without having to hook a single ball, since, on our put-in to the scrum, we adopted the French tactic of just walking over the ball, one of the lessons that we had learnt from our earlier matches in Europe. An added bonus for us that afternoon was that Graham Henry, who had come specifically to Ireland to see the game, called in our changing room after the match to congratulate us on a fine performance. Unfortunately, Leinster took their revenge in the corresponding fixture at Stradey and we also lost the away games against the two French teams in our pool.

During these matches, the tendons in my right knee had been very painful and because putting my whole weight on it, particularly when running, was very uncomfortable I began to 'carry' it a little. As a result I started to get an acute pain in my groin, which I found difficult to bear. The Llanelli club decided to send me to see Dr Gilmour at a private clinic in London. He was renowned in the sporting world as an expert in the treatment of that particular injury which, in his view, was so common that every professional rugby and soccer player should consider receiving treatment with the specific aim of strengthening the groin. As it happened Duncan Ferguson, the Everton striker, was at the clinic at the same time as me and for the same reason. I was able to walk from the clinic the day following surgery but I wasn't able to train for a further six weeks, with the result that, naturally, my fitness level had dropped considerably during that period. At that time also I had to be very careful with regard to my daily duties with SWALEC and avoid climbing poles and ladders.

I was desperately keen to return and lead Llanelli in the race for the Welsh Championship. We'd been doing well all through the season and although winning the Welsh Cup the previous year had been a great feeling for us, the big test was to show that we could sustain the consistency that was required to win a season-long competition. We did just that and it was particularly pleasing for me to win the Welsh Cup in my first year as captain and then the Welsh Championship at the end of my second year. During the second part of that season it had been a great boost for us to see John Davies, the prop from Boncath, returning from the Richmond club to play for the Scarlets. I was so pleased to see him joining us at Stradey, firstly because he was an old friend from the time we used to compete in the Strongest Man in Wales television series. Secondly, our front row became much stronger as a result and he continued to have a huge impact on that aspect of play over a lengthy period.

But there was to be no Welsh Cup success that year since we were comprehensively beaten 10-37 by Swansea in the final at Ninian Park. One of the reasons for our defeat was that by May we were a very tired team. We had to play two games a week towards the end of the season, mainly because of postponed games resulting from our reaching the last eight in the Heineken competition, and this intensive period took its toll.

Another honour that came my way that month was returning to Menai Bridge to officially open the new Menai Bridge Rugby Club field and clubhouse. To celebrate the occasion a game had been arranged between the club's first team and a President's XV and it was a great feeling to turn out again alongside friends who'd been fellow players during our youth, like Trystan Williams and Huw Percy. The game itself was a very pleasing experience, as was the whole day's activity, and I was very glad of the opportunity to be able to repay, in some small way, stalwarts such as Wil Williams, who was now President of the Club, and Doug Barnes, along with many others who'd given me such excellent support during my early career. The occasion was also important as it gave me another opportunity to maintain my links with Anglesey. I have welcomed every chance to return there ever since I settled in south Wales and it has been a privilege to receive, on more than one occasion, a special award from the Isle of Anglesey Council for my contribution to the world of sport. Likewise, in September 1999, it was a pleasure to accept an invitation to open the new clubhouse at Llangefni Rugby Club.

Yet there was one great disappointment to come my way at the end of the 1998-99 season. Despite our success during my period as the Llanelli captain Gareth Jenkins was of the opinion that the game against Swansea in the final of the Cup had taken a lot out of me. He decided therefore that Wayne Proctor should be captain the following season, since he'd been a regular member of the first team for many years. At the time I didn't think that such criteria should be used for selecting a captain, bearing in mind the importance that Gareth attached to the sense of privilege every player should feel when wearing the scarlet shirt, particularly the captain's mantle. I'm sure he would have appreciated the disappointment I felt on losing that particular honour.

Rugby was, by now, a more professional game on many levels. Standards were higher, with much more attention being given to tactics, fitness and power and there were also greater demands on the players. As a result I decided, at the close of the 1998-99 season, to ask Western Power to release me from my work on Wednesdays, since it was the only full day's training scheduled by Llanelli. The person who gave me permission to implement this arrangement was Phil Davies, my boss at Llanfihangel-ar-arth and later at Pontarddulais and I am grateful to him for the extremely fair way in which he treated me during my time with Western Power. A few weeks later the company began to consider the possibility of having to lay off staff, which at the time was a matter of some concern to my colleagues. At Union gatherings I would usually be very quiet but when we arranged to meet with management to discuss the matter I voiced my concern that I feared that the Company had a hidden agenda to introduce private contractors to increasingly undertake work that would normally be done by the gang. Perhaps I felt at the time, in view of the way rugby was progressing, that I had less to lose than the other lads by speaking out and, hopefully, advancing their case.

I have to confess that the extra full-day's training made a big difference to my fitness and I could feel that those sessions were now bringing the best out of me. I have always taken to asking others, during strenuous fitness sessions, how much benefit they derived from the challenges with which we were presented. There would be no point in my addressing such a question to Steve Ford or Martyn Madden, since they considered every training session to be extremely strenuous! As a guideline to my personal fitness I preferred to ask players like Simon Easterby, who was always totally professional in his approach to training and preparation. Meic Griffith at Menai Bridge Rugby Club had given me an important early lesson in this particular context, which I remember to this day. His words were: "Don't ever show the bloke in charge of fitness that he's had the better of you. Show that you're always ready for more!" But it hasn't always been easy to follow that advice!

Despite all the hard work I put in to try and ensure that I was ready for the 1999-2000 season I suffered a big disappointment in the first match against Ebbw Vale. I injured my knee and was consequently out of the game for weeks. However, there were some exercises that I could do in the meantime, for example, drills to increase my upper body strength and blowing periodically into a purpose-built machine to increase my lung capacity. At the same time I was receiving continual treatment to the injury itself, under the capable hands of Dai Chips, or, to those not familiar with Llanelli Rugby Club, Dai Jenkins, the physiotherapist at Stradey and one of the club characters. Dai got to discover everything about everybody directly from the treatment room bed and no-one at Stradey knew more about the players than him. This is true of most physios and I know how important a contribution Mark Davies has made to the Wales set-up over the years and how much club coaches have profited from his work.

That autumn, of course, we had the excitement of the World Cup in Wales but I had no contribution to make to the Wales campaign, which turned out, unfortunately, to be rather disappointing. But I was part of the excellent Llanelli run in the Heineken Cup that year. We got a great result in Bourgoin at the Pool stage, being the first Welsh team to win in France in that particular competition; we beat Ulster in addition. However, perhaps the most memorable encounter that year was our win over Wasps at Stradey in an electrifying match. I particularly remember Scott Quinnell storming through, having flattened Lawrence Dallaglio, and then Craig Gilles galloping along the touchline to score, thus ensuring a ten point victory margin to enable us to proceed to the next round. Lawrence, at one point, lost his head completely, after being teased by Ian Boobyer. This was one of Ian's attributes on the field, if he was on your side! He was also a practical joker off it and I remember one incident in particular when John Davies had been avidly reading a particular book for some time only to find, when he came towards the end, that Ian had ripped out the final chapter!

We proceeded to the last eight of the Heineken Cup and registered a win against Cardiff, only to suffer the heartbreak of losing 28–31 to Northampton in the semi-final. Paul Grayson kicked a penalty during injury time to secure the victory, after Ian Boobyer had been penalised for kicking the ball out of the hands of Don Malone, the scrum-half who came on as a replacement for Matt Dawson. Needless to say old Ian took a lot of stick from the lads as a result! The weather was so hot on that particular day that all the players immersed their heads in buckets of iced water during half time, in an effort to reduce their body temperature. It was perhaps just as well that we didn't have to play extra time!

What I remember most, apart from Stephen Jones kicking 23 points, was the magnificent backing we got from our supporters. As we travelled by coach to the ground all we could see on the surrounding streets were thousands of Northampton supporters enthusiastically waving their flags, which made me worry that perhaps support for the Scarlets that afternoon was going to be pretty thin. However, as the bus turned in to the stadium car park, the far end, where the beer tents were located, was one mass of scarlet and the fervent support of the Llanelli followers was an inspiration to us throughout the match. The Scarlets fans are renowned for their support at Stradey of course but the passion and the enthusiasm they displayed on that occasion, just as at Nottingham for our game against Leicester in the semi-final of the Heineken Cup in 2002, still remain with me to this day.

Losing to Northampton was a huge disappointment but beating Swansea in the final of the Welsh Cup at the Millennium Stadium was some kind of consolation. That was the first time that I had played there and I must say it's one of the best locations that I've ever experienced. Facilities for supporters and players are excellent and I like the idea of being able to close the roof during wet weather. Some people favour letting the elements take their toll in games there but in my opinion there's no satisfaction in playing or winning a match with the roof open during atrocious weather.

The international season also finished on an encouraging note as I was chosen as reserve to Garin for the Wales team's final Six Nations game in Dublin. During half-time, while Graham Henry was addressing the team in the changing room, Neil Jenkins and I took a ball around a corner and kicked it quietly back and fore to each other. Ironically, with fifteen minutes remaining of the second half both of us were required to take the field.

Soon afterwards, with Wales losing 17–19, Neil ran the ball from his own 22 before passing it to me. Unusually for me I put in a grubber kick and began running. Realistically I didn't have much hope of getting to the ball first but Keith Wood held me back during the chase. Neil kicked the penalty goal that we were awarded as a result of that offence, to put us in the lead and, shortly afterwards, he kicked another, to seal the victory for us by 23–19. That practice session that Neil and I had during the interval must have paid off! Wales finished fourth in the Championship that season after gaining three victories. I had by now won my fourth international cap.

Yet the main event of the season had taken place in February, namely the birth of our second son, Harry. It was a very happy occasion, of course, but not without its problems. Because Billy's birth two years previously had been difficult for Tina she had decided in advance that Harry would came into this world by means of a Caesarean birth. Although that, in itself, hadn't been a problem, both Tina and I sensed at the time that all was not well and that the medical staff at Glangwili Hospital were a little worried. To make matters worse the doctor asked us if we were aware that there was a tumour. It was all very complicated and a matter of some concern at the time. In due course we were informed that a fibroid tumour the size of a melon had grown in Tina's womb. She was told that she would have to return to the hospital once she had regained strength after the birth. She duly had the tumour removed and had no further complications.

At the start of the 2001-2 season I felt I was playing better than ever and was keen to put myself to the test at international level. In the sessions that were held as part of the national squad's fitness programme I remember making quite an impression on Graham Henry with regard to my fitness level. Yet I was selected for the A team in the two international matches that had been arranged that autumn, against South Africa A and New Zealand

A, coached at the time by Steve Hansen. But, before that, Graham had a word with me to explain how he thought I could contribute to the squad. He'd also made me captain for both games, which I considered to be quite an honour. By this time the Wales A team was getting the respect it deserved and preparations for its games were given the same attention as those of the national team. We would now meet six days before a match at the Vale Hotel where we would practice, discuss tactics, hold press conferences, have meetings between senior players and coaching staff and enjoy relaxing together. In the midst of all this activity we would be given one afternoon and night off to return home to be with our families until the following morning.

Despite losing those two A team games I thought that I'd played rather well myself and that I'd led the boys with some success. Apparently the lineout statistics, in particular, had made quite an impression on Graham Henry. After the two matches each member of the Welsh squad received a written report from Graham, assessing every aspect of his particular game. I welcomed this development since it put down a marker with regard to where I stood in the eyes of the coach. I got a very favourable report but it noted that I was still the third choice in the hooker hierarchy, behind Garin and, by this time, Andrew Lewis, a Cardiff prop who could also play hooker. I had no complaints concerning Garin's status but the second choice for the hooker position spurred me on to make an even greater effort to get to the top.

Llanelli's experience of the European Cup that season was disappointing as we failed to progress beyond the Pool games. The highlight of the season for me, however, was playing for Wales against England at the Millennium Stadium, on February 3rd, 2001. After seven years in the wilderness, as it were, following my first cap in Fiji, I was at last selected to start a match in the Six Nations Championship. It was no wonder that I regarded that cap as my first proper cap and judging by the response I received from family and friends, in the form of cards and innumerable telephone calls, there were many others who thought likewise.

By this time I had accepted that it was my own fault that I'd been ignored for such a long time. I hadn't appreciated the opportunities that came my way, hadn't adopted the right attitude nor had I questioned myself as to why I wasn't being selected and what could I do about that. I was too ready to criticise, with the result that I now feel embarrassed concerning some of the comments that I made to all and sundry. So, because I had wasted that first opportunity many years previously, I was now determined to make the most of my chance. Yet I wouldn't have changed anything since I managed to learn lessons from those earlier experiences, which proved to be invaluable during the rest of my playing career. I now felt that I had command over my own game and sensed that Graham Henry, too, had considerable faith in me. Knowing that did both my confidence and my attitude a power of good.

My way of approaching that game against England was no different to the way I would prepare for such a match throughout my subsequent international career. A big meal on the Friday night and then a trip to the cinema with the rest of the squad, something which still happens and which has been the custom for many, many years. In those days it was like a school outing. Everybody would arrive at the multiplex cinema together, by coach, with Trevor James, the national squad manager at the time, leading the way. Then he, poor chap, would have to buy the tickets for the whole party, escort everyone to his seat and distribute all the Cornettos during the intermission! This pattern changed during my final years as a player, with the boys being allowed to visit the cinema as they wished, usually in their own cars and in their own clothes.

I slept soundly that Friday night and woke early the following morning. I tried not to think too much about the game ahead since that usually tended to make me feel a little tired. Then I got up about ten thirty and ate a hearty breakfast of bacon, scrambled eggs and brown sauce with tea and toast. I would then eat nothing else until after the game. Back to my room straight afterwards where I was happy enough to be on my own. Indeed sometimes I felt the need to be alone was perhaps a throwback from those years when I spent all that time training on my own and living away from home after leaving north Wales.

The coach journey to the centre of Cardiff through the thousands upon thousands of supporters into the bowels of the Stadium was indeed memorable and served to whet my appetite to get to grips with England as soon as possible. My parents were somewhere in the crowd but they'd been rather apprehensive about attending the game for, during the period approaching that particular day, they'd begun to think that they brought with them some kind of jinx, since I got injured almost every time they came to see me play.

Playing in the hooker's position for England that day was Dorian West who'd been born in Wrexham and whose parents came from Ynysybwl, which was Garin country of course. In fact Garin had played for Swansea against him the previous weekend so he gave me the lowdown on the Leicester hooker. "Nothing to worry about" was his message and that's how it turned out as far as the front row battle was concerned. However, England thrashed us 44–15, which was a huge disappointment for both Welsh players and supporters and we had to admit that a far superior team had beaten us on the day. It was important for me that I had a decent match since I considered it to be a 'second chance' game. I kept my place for the next outing against Scotland and, as we walked around Murrayfield on the preceding Friday, Graham Henry came up to me and said that, although I was new to that particular team, in his opinion I'd already created a big impression and that he considered me to be one of his most experienced players, words which were of course a great comfort to me. The match ended 25–25 although we'd been ahead 25–6 at one stage. The Ireland game that season was cancelled because of the foot and mouth outbreak and we beat Italy quite easily. But the highlight of the season was undoubtedly the excellent victory over France in Paris. Travelling by coach from the team hotel to Stade Français is an unique experience, behind an escort of a number of police outriders. Any vehicle that might hinder or obstruct the coach in some way is given an impatient kick as they pass and if they consider travelling on the wrong side of the road to be more expedient then they expect the coach to do likewise, regardless of how dangerous that might be!

We were never in any danger of losing that game against France, which we won 35–43. We did better than expected in the lineouts and the scrums, where I felt completely comfortable packing down between Dai Young and Darren Morris. Graham Henry was so pleased with the performance that he presented each of our players with a video copy of the game, as a record of the positive steps we had taken as a team and as a blueprint of what he was trying to get us to achieve.

Before the France match my name had been announced amongst a group of 67 players that were being considered for the Lions tour to Australia that summer. Throughout my career I had been used to seeing my name being omitted from various teams so that particular selection came as a complete surprise and I didn't think for a moment that I would end up being in the final squad. It was, therefore, quite a shock to discover that I had in fact been chosen, on April 25, 2001, to be in the party of 37 that would be making the trip 'down under'. From being third choice for Wales in November 2000, I was now one of three hookers, along with Keith Wood and Phil Greening, who were considered to be the best in Britain. I think that I was literally up a pole when I heard on the radio that I had been selected. Indeed the customer for whom I was doing that job at the time took a photograph of me at the top of the pole, with the caption "Guess where Robin McBryde was when he heard of his selection for the British Lions!"

Having gratefully received the congratulatory messages that came from here, there and everywhere it was then time to try and sort out a few practical problems that would result from an overseas trip lasting many weeks. Tina had already assured me that she and the boys would be fine. However, one matter that needed to be resolved immediately was my position within Western Power. As soon as I had walked through the door of Phil Davies's office, he, as my boss, knew immediately what I wanted. After a friendly chat it was agreed that I would take sabbatical leave for a period of one year. That suited me well since it would enable me to go on the Lions tour and then, on my return from Australia, to experience life for a while as a full-time professional rugby player. In any event some difficulties had arisen lately regarding the need to balance my duty to my employer and my obligations to the Wales squad. Indeed, on some occasions, it had been necessary for my mates at work to cover for me, which, in fairness, they did quietly and willingly. There remained one small matter that needed sorting out. Billy, who was now a little over three years old, said that he didn't at all fancy seeing his father turning into a lion!

# CHAPTER 9

# A Troubled Lion

Adversity introduces a man to himself.

**Anon**

THE LIONS SQUAD got together towards the end of May 2001, at Tylney Hall in Hampshire, before flying to Perth a week later. The Coach for the tour was Graham Henry, with the Irishman, Donald Lenihan, a former Lion himself, as Manager of the party. The aim of that residential period was to enable the players to get to know each other and the management team to discover more about us. In addition to questionnaires a number of practical tests were held so that the management team and us, as players, could obtain some indication of our physical and mental durability.

One of the first tasks we were given was to write, on a flip-chart, answers to specific questions, which were then discussed when we were later divided into groups. The leader of our discussion group happened to be Graham. For a joke, on one side of the chart, I wrote some tongue-in-cheek answers while on the other side I took the questions seriously and provided genuine answers. Therefore, on the side that Graham would see first, to the question 'In what kind of situations do you feel least comfortable?' I had written, 'When I meet strangers in unfamiliar surroundings'. To the question 'What do you hate doing most?' I replied, 'Establishing new relationships and travelling overseas'. Naturally Graham began to look rather dismayed as he went through my 'false' replies and probably thought that he'd selected one of life's anti-social creatures to be one of Britain's rugby ambassadors to Australia.

However, I found nothing amusing about the next task that we were set. Each player had to stand before his particular group and talk about himself for some minutes. In other words it provided an opportunity for everyone to elaborate on his comments on the chart and, in my particular case, on the genuine comments. It was obvious that some members of the group were very familiar with that kind of situation but for Martyn Williams and myself, it was a nightmare scenario. To make matters worse the person in our group who spoke immediately before us was Lawrence Dallaglio, who announced that one of his pet hates was people who had no confidence in themselves. However, since both Lawrence and Austin Healy, the 'Leicester Lip', were in our group there wasn't time for Martyn and myself to say much! One member of the management team, Steve Black, really enjoyed that kind of session, with the result that his group carried on with their discussions for literally hours. Blackie's role on the tour was that of 'conditioner', someone who was supposed to make everybody else feel good about themselves and I must say he was an expert at it. He'd been a member of the Wales coaching team for many years until his departure in 2000, which was a great disappointment for many of us players. Unfortunately, as I shall explain later, I had cause to depend a great deal on Blackie's particular talents during the forthcoming tour.

A great deal of emphasis was placed on the importance of 'bonding' in the tour preparations. I have, by now, had experience of being part of the management team on overseas tours and I have to confess that such sessions have their merits, within reason. Prior to my stay at Tylney Hall I had attended just one 'bonding' camp, with Llanelli, at the army training centre in Poole. We were split into teams of eight to undertake a number of physical tasks. We were despatched to surrounding areas, taking with us logs, water and a stretcher. En route it was planned that we would be confronted with an accident, featuring bodies and blood everywhere, with the result that some of the team were already beginning to wilt. Then we were expected to row a boat to a nearby island, and then follow a map in order to get to a particular location. On the way there, so that we could cook ourselves a meal at a later stage, we had to pick up supplies, which constituted a bag of potatoes here a sack of carrots there and then a chicken. The problem was that the chicken was alive. The meal was to be cooked in a specific camp at the end of our trek. After walking for hours, we thought that we were almost there ... until we spotted the camp, miles away across country. We eventually got there, by which time we were all starving and a Sergeant Major appeared to show us what we needed to do with the chicken, which was to kill it by quickly screwing its neck. This alone proved too much for some players who had grown quite attached to the chicken– even giving it its own name! One of the players, who played centre, volunteered for the job but he overestimated the amount of force that was required to do the job. The next thing we noticed was that he was standing there with the chicken's head in one hand and its body in the other ... and it was still alive! At this point Neil Boobyer and Martyn Madden, usually very hearty eaters, decided that they weren't hungry after all. In due course we were shown how to pluck the chicken and how to open it up to remove the eggs so that we could eat them as well. By that time hardly any of us felt like eating! And after all that, before we could settle down for the night, we had to pitch our tents. During the early hours one group had to get up in order to reposition their tent since the tide had come in further than they had estimated; we also had to move because we'd pitched our tent on an ants' nest! All this was aimed at showing how we reacted under pressure to various situations and to demonstrate who amongst us was 'leader' material. Did it, however, I ask myself, equip us to be better rugby players?

I was aware at the beginning of the Lions tour that I was the third choice hooker. Yet Andy Robinson, who was in charge of the forwards, told me that he saw things differently and that he expected me to fight for my place in the Test team. That gave me a lot of encouragement as I was very conscious of the fact that I was quite a 'new boy' to many on the tour. For example, James Robson, the Scotsman who was the Lions' official doctor, had no idea who I was when I went to see him for the first time. In the beginning there were eighteen England players in the party (most of whom thought they had a special right to be there), ten Welshmen, six Irishmen and three Scotsmen. The first players from the other three countries that I got to know fairly well were Jason Leonard (I shared a room with him at Tylney Hall) and Rob Henderson, after having decided to go for a pint together one night before leaving for Australia.

I enjoyed our first few days 'down under' in Manly, near Sydney. It was a great place to stay and training was going well. Some aspects were rather complicated at the start but we Welsh players had a slight advantage over the others in the party in that Graham Henry had decided to resort to the same tactics during loose play as we used when playing for Wales, for example, with regard to the positions to be adopted in rucks and mauls and following scrums and lineouts. That is, a 'pod' system would be operated, which I shall discuss in greater detail later. It was great to see so many Welsh supporters out there, with the lads from the other three countries being taken aback somewhat by the familiarity which seemed to exist between the Welsh players and their supporters. Unfortunately, during training for the first game, rather a serious problem reared its head. Phil Greening, one of the hookers, was hurt so badly that he was told immediately that he would be taking no further part on the tour. Nevertheless, he decided to stay on until the end of the trip because he had sponsors who were willing to pay for him. Once the seriousness of his injury had been confirmed a call went out to Gordon Bulloch, the Scottish hooker, who was on holiday at the time, to join the party.

I had an early taste of playing for the Lions during our first game against Western Australia in Perth, when I came on as a replacement for Keith Wood, with ten minutes of the game remaining. The opposition were all amateur players with the result that there was a huge difference between the two teams. In a match that resembled a training session we scored 18 tries as we romped home 116–10. When I was selected to start the second game, against the Queensland President's Fifteen in Townsville, I felt really chuffed, but within seven minutes of the kick-off I got an injury which turned the tour into the biggest nightmare of my rugby career.

As I ran to offer support in open play I received an accidental kick on the thigh by one of the opposition who had dived in to make a tackle. I thought at first that some running about would get rid of the pain and that I would be able to play on, particularly since Gordon Bulloch, who was on the bench, had only just arrived in Australia. Before long, however, I was unable to walk properly, let alone play. By the time I left the field I couldn't bend my leg at all. I was prepared to accept that the injury was nothing more than a severe case of dead leg but when I had a scan the following morning it showed that there was a large haematoma there.

During the next few days, while the other lads were training and visiting the local sights, I was tied to the hotel. I was receiving treatment regularly from the two physiotherapists, one being the Welsh physio, Carcus (Mark Davies) from Swansea. The only exercises I could manage to facilitate bending the leg were a little swimming, walking up and down the stairs, and riding a static bike in the gym. I was feeling quite disheartened by now and it was at this particular point that Steve Black came to my rescue.

One day he took me to a bookshop in Manly and handed me a couple of volumes for me to have a look at. Perhaps this will be difficult to take in but, up until then, I had never in my life read a book from beginning to end, since I had no interest whatsoever in reading. I preferred spending my leisure time actually *doing* something or *going* somewhere. But Blackie had chosen, for my attention, a book in the series *Chicken Soup*, entitled *Chicken Soup for the Soul*. Ever since that particular day I've been an avid reader, with a taste for all kinds of books, thanks to that particular volume, which really helped me to put things in perspective, despite my disappointment at the time. Indeed, I was extremely grateful to Blackie for the valuable support that I received from him during that unhappy period.

After a week or so the leg improved and the haematoma began to go down. The coaching team therefore decided to give me a fitness test on the eve of the game against Australia A on June 25th. They made me run back and fore along the beach at Manly but I knew that the leg wasn't right. Yet I was under quite a bit of pressure to play in that game, pressure created by myself in the main, since there were all kinds of issues at the time which had a bearing on how I regarded my situation. I knew that the management team had a problem, following the injury to Phil Greening and due to the fact that Gordon Bulloch hadn't yet had time to find his feet. I also knew that my parents were about to arrive in Australia to follow the Lions during the last few weeks of the tour so I wanted to attain an acceptable level of fitness by the time they arrived. In addition, an old friend from Bangor, Gavin McClennan, who had married a girl from New Zealand and had settled in that country, had travelled to Australia to see me play. All things considered I felt that I should take the field against Australia A, despite the fact that I knew in my heart that I wasn't 100 per cent fit.

I was given a special pair of shorts to wear in the game,

with a hole in the centre of the leg, surrounded with some thick material, and I was instructed to be particularly careful. Yet I was far from happy during the game. Apart from the fact that I wasn't feeling very well our play as a team left a lot to be desired. The lineouts, in particular, were a shambles and I was told years later by Scott Johnson that the Australian coaching team had by that time cracked the code we were using when throwing in. We were constantly penalised at the scrum for various offences, although we had the obvious advantage. The result was that, after an hour, Gordon Bulloch replaced me, although that had no bearing on the team performance for the remainder of the match. We lost 25–28 and I wasn't at all happy with the condition of my leg, nor with my performance.

I was selected to be on the bench for our next game, four days later, against New South Wales Waratahs in Sydney. I was glad about that, despite the dodgy state of my leg, since my parents had arrived by this time and there was a chance, therefore, that they would get to see me play in a Lions jersey. I was glad too of the opportunity of meeting them in Manly following their journey there by ferryboat from Sydney. My mother was celebrating her birthday so I took her to buy a present ... a copy of *Chicken Soup for the Soul*!

I was the only Welsh-speaking member of the Lions squad at the time, since Scott Gibbs didn't arrive until later, so I was the only one available to do interviews for the Welsh-language media. I tried to remain positive concerning my injury and would frequently maintain that I expected to be fully fit before long. However, I wasn't telling the truth since I knew deep down that the situation was quite bad. I came on for the last ten minutes of a very hard game against the Waratahs, which we won 41–24. The occasion will be mostly remembered for the merciless pounding to the face of Ronan O'Gara from Duncan MacRae, the home team full back, as he lay on the ground. During the short time that I was on the field I received another painful blow to the leg. The situation was not looking good.

I consulted the physios regarding my injury, and their opinion was that they didn't think I would play again during the tour. By this time the leg was completely stiff and the haematoma had moved lower down. Naturally, perhaps, I was feeling pretty low and the world about me appeared rather bleak. We'd moved on to stay at the luxurious Novotel Hotel in Coffs Harbour, where the Lions were going to play against the NSW Country Cockatoos, and I got a very pleasant surprise. As I stood on our training pitch there who should walk across the field towards me but Meic Griffith who'd travelled as a backpacker to Australia to follow the Lions. It was great to have his company for a while, and he accepted my parents' invitation to travel with them in their rented car to Brisbane for the First Test.

During our stay at the hotel, I had one of the most harrowing experiences of my life on the beach nearby. My injury did not permit me to do much apart from going for a stroll every now and again along the beach, and on one such occasion a young girl came running towards me shouting that a man was lying at the water's edge and that he had drowned. She continued running to the hotel to seek help while I made my way towards the small group of people who were standing around the lifeless person on the sand. They were young surfers who had made their way ashore when they saw a body in the water. When I got there one of them was trying to resuscitate him using the 'kiss of life' method. Since I had received some first-aid training in connection with my job, I began pumping his chest, until a lifeguard arrived from the hotel and took over.

As I stepped back to give him room to work I noticed, for the first time, that the person lying there was wearing the same kind of swimming kit as had been issued to the members of the Lions party. I saw that it was Anton Toia, the pleasant and popular Maori that the Australian Rugby Union had appointed as our liaison officer, to look after the needs of the Lions party during the tour. He'd been on a boat trip with some of the squad, who had then decided to go on to another location across the bay. Anton, however, since he wished to return to the hotel, had decided to swim from the boat to the beach. Unfortunately, as he was swimming to the shore, he had suffered a heart attack. He died on the beach.

I had decided, by this time, that I wanted to return home and I telephoned my parents to tell them. This came as a shattering blow for my mother while my father, too, was quite dejected. The fact that they were staying at the time in the Byron Bay Hotel, one of the 25 foremost hotels in the world, did little to alleviate their disappointment. They'd planned and made reservations for the following two weeks of the tour, so they had no other choice but to continue their journey, although their original reason for doing so was to see me represent the British Lions. I had to stay and see the lads play the First Test and I was so pleased for them when they won that game 29–13, after an excellent performance.

But the big story of the day was that Matt Dawson had written an article, in the form of a diary, published in Britain that morning in *The Daily Telegraph*, which was critical of the way in which the management team treated the Lions players on the tour. He claimed that many of them wanted to pack it in and return home since the tour was a 'disaster'. None of the Lions players were aware of this until after the Test match and I clearly remember Matt Dawson, who was one of the substitutes that afternoon, coming into the changing room after the final whistle, where everyone else was celebrating, and holding his head in his hands. He, no doubt, realised then the extent of his foolishness, which had occurred only a short time before the magnificent achievement of his fellow players in that First Test.

The management team were naturally disappointed and angry that Matt had resorted to such action and he was obliged to pay a heavy fine and appear before the whole party, in sackcloth and ashes, to apologise.

I must confess that I hadn't been aware of any tension between management and players. It's true that the mid-week team had a grumble a few days before the First Test. Graham Henry expected them to operate as defenders against the Lions Test team in one of the training session while they thought that they should be allowed to pursue their own practice plans in readiness for their game against the NSW Cockatoos the following day. I remember them running around the pitch singing '*Sloop John B*' and finishing each verse with a 'tongue-in-cheek' refrain, "*This is the worst tour we've ever been on*"! I was given to understand that Graham Henry lost the support of a number of players during the remainder of the tour but, although I was by that time following proceedings from my armchair at home, he had my sympathies.

It wasn't an easy tour, with a fixture list of ten games, three of which were Test matches, in five weeks. There were 37 players champing at the bit to play, many of whom, particularly members of the England team, thought that they should be in the Test team every time. Indeed the tour was damaged further when another damning newspaper article appeared, this time written by Austin Healy, who was also fined. Yet I remember talking to him some time afterwards when he admitted that he had done well from the publicity that resulted from that particular incident, and that his agent had never been busier! Austin was always full of himself but what made him different to many others of a similar nature was that he had the personal skills to sustain his outgoing and self-confident personality. For example, when the lads would be teasing each other concerning their golfing prowess Austin could drive the ball off the tee by running at it from four or five yards and belting it down the fairway. Similarly he could go on his knees and hit the ball cleanly from that position too!

I said goodbye to my parents following the First Test in Brisbane. They continued with their journey, with my mother, according to my father at the time, in tears at the start of each one of the remaining five games as she realised that they were at the far end of the world while I, by that time, was at home in Tumble. Scott Quinnell kindly went to meet them at the airport in Canberra and saw to it that they had tickets for each of those games. I stayed in Brisbane for a day or two, along with Lawrence Dallaglio, who also had to return home because of injury, before we flew back to Britain together. While in Brisbane I had a chance to spend a very pleasant day with Salesi Finau, since he lived nearby. In addition, Lawrence had many business connections in the city, which meant that we were well looked after while we were there. He, too, was, of course, very disappointed that he had to miss the rest of the tour. Despite the unfortunate, brash image that he has in the eyes of many Welsh people he was a very pleasant travelling companion on what was a tiresome journey in many ways. On top of everything my leg was quite painful and, to make matters worse, I was unable to bend it. Every time I needed to go to the toilet during the flight back to Britain I had to leave the toilet door open, with my leg sticking straight out!

It was difficult to accept at the time but I'm sure that there's a reason for everything that happens, even the bad luck that came my way on the Lions tour. Despite suffering disappointment and dismay I think I learned a great deal from the experience, both as a player and as a person.

# CHAPTER 10

# The All Black Influence

Strength and weakness have nothing to do with courage
or muscle; only recognition. Strong people recognise their
weakness. They also recognise their ability to overcome those
weaknesses. Weak people deny their weaknesses, and fail to
recognise how strong they truly are.

**Carmen Mariano**

I WAS BY now a full-time professional player having signed
a three-year contract with the Scarlets. Initially I missed
the stability of following a regular work schedule as I had
been doing for the previous fifteen years. It even felt strange
to go out in the morning without my beloved lunch-box but,
in due course, I settled effortlessly into my new occupation.
Of course the world of professional rugby was new to the
Llanelli club as well. As a result we players were expected at
first to come in every day and, for the whole day, to practice,
work on fitness and discuss tactics. Nowadays it is accepted
that players need sufficient rest to keep them fresh and alert,
in body and in spirit, so it is common practice for players to
be given two days off following a match.

It was strange having to play for Wales in a Six Nations game
in the middle of October but that's what happened in Cardiff in
2001 when we met Ireland in a fixture that had been postponed
the previous winter because of the foot and mouth outbreak. We
were well beaten, 6–36, and I have the bitter memory of going,
along with the rest of the team, to the Park Hotel for the post-
match dinner and being booed by our supporters as we came off
the bus. For me it was a new and miserable experience.

By this time Steve Hansen, a New Zealander, had joined

the coaching team as an assistant to Graham Henry and was specifically responsible for coaching the forwards, despite the fact that Lyn Howells, the Pontypridd coach, was already engaged in that role. Steve was not an easy person to get to know in the beginning as he came across at times as being rather reserved, dour and stubborn. He brought with him a new system for throwing in at the lineout which, at first, was not at all popular with the forwards. He wanted the hookers to throw the ball into space, with the jumpers timing their jump so as to meet the ball at the peak of its path through the air. I remember doubts being cast at the time as to Steve's qualifications to coach the forwards since we had found out that he had spent his playing career in the centre. When he saw how disenchanted Andy Moore, our main jumper, and I were with the new system he showed a video of the Canterbury pack, whom he had coached previously, using it with a great deal of success. Our explanation for this was that none of the opposition jumpers in the *Super 12* would contest the throw when it was Canterbury ball, to which Steve replied that the opposition forwards were not challenging the Canterbury jumpers because, as a result of the system that he had introduced, they had no idea where the ball was going to be thrown. Yet his message to me was, *"Carry on throwing into space; if we don't win the ball, carry on doing it. I know that you know what we're trying to do"*. That advice wasn't easy to follow, especially in front of a 70,000 crowd in the Millennium Stadium baying for your blood!

We played three more games that autumn in Cardiff, against Argentina, Australia and Tonga. We lost the first two, having played poorly, and beat Tonga easily. The Argentina match saw Iestyn Harries making his debut in a Welsh shirt but, as was the case with regard to his whole career with the national team, people expected much more from him than he could offer so soon after his transfer from Rugby League. There's no doubt, however, that he was an extremely talented player. I remember one particular training session when Steve Hansen, after being appointed the national coach, tried to show the forwards how to deal with footwork when tackling. In the drill that we adopted, each of the players, in turn, had to tackle an attacker running at them within a very narrow channel. When it was Gareth Llewellyn's turn to try and stop Iestyn he failed to get anywhere near him as the newcomer danced past him, despite the limited space available to him. *"No! No!"* was Steve's response, *"not like that, Gareth, like this!"*, as he then stood in for the defender in order to show him how he should have stopped Iestyn. But the same thing happened again, and again, (and again!) as Steve was left clutching air. I don't think he was a fan of Iestyn's talent at that particular moment. Unfortunately Welsh rugby supporters weren't given an opportunity to really appreciate his skills, mainly because he was pushed into the cauldron of Union international rugby far too early. Off the pitch he was very tolerant and maintained his sense of humour – no mean feat bearing in mind all the banter he had to take in the changing room because of his pronounced northern England accent!

Our Heineken Cup campaign with the Scarlets began at the end of September when we lost 9–12 at Leicester. The highlight of the game for me was preventing Andy Goode from scoring a try with a chest-high tackle that flattened him and left him quite shaken. It was one of those occasions where I had enough time to set up the tackle in my mind before launching myself at him from his blind side. There was a question as to whether I came from an offside position, but I wasn't going to stop and ask when the opportunity presented itself! There are always tackles that stick in your mind, both in giving and receiving the so-called 'big hits', so, when the chance comes, you make the most of it.

Putting down a marker in the early part of any match can instil trepidation amongst the opposing team and can have a demoralising effect on their confidence and ultimately on their game. It can also have a huge impact in raising your own levels of confidence early on in a game and the old saying of 'first impressions count' could never be more true. During Wales's opening match against Canada in the 2003 World Cup, their prop Rod Snow ran straight at me with one of his trademark charges up the field. I didn't have to move much, which meant that I was in a good position to stop him in his tracks, which I did, and followed it up with a few words of comfort for him. I was never one to give 'verbal' during games, but because of the occasion and importance of the match I couldn't contain myself and it gave me a huge boost. On that note, I'm firmly convinced that not enough emphasis is placed on the psychological aspects when preparing players for the modern game, especially in our academy structure. Time is spent on developing their physiques and skill levels, both important aspects obviously, but if they are unable to transfer all that investment on to the pitch due to a weakness in their mental approach it is all in vain. I know that some still regard going to a psychologist as a sign of weakness, and it's true to say that it isn't for everyone, but it should never be completely ignored. What is needed is a player who reacts well under pressure or following a setback and there is no doubt that Wales is littered with examples of wasted talent partly because players are content to play within their own comfort zone where they are rarely tested to their full potential.

Anyhow, we took revenge on Leicester at Stradey, winning 24–12 (with Stephen Jones kicking eight penalty goals and Andy Goode getting four) and assisted by the passionate support of the home crowd. On this occasion, however, Gareth had taken us for the customary warm-up to our practice pitch nearby, as opposed to Stradey itself, in front of the spectators, as was our normal practice. As a result, that first roar by the crowd as we took the field almost raised the roof, which served to inspire us for the whole game. In the other pool games we beat Calvisano twice and won against Perpignan at home and, although we were thrashed in the return game in France, we'd done enough to proceed to the quarter-finals which entailed playing away against Bath in January.

That was a memorable journey for many reasons. After heavy rain on the Saturday, the Irish referee, Alan Lewis, decided at 1.15 p.m. that it would not be possible to play the game that afternoon. By that time, thousands of Llanelli supporters had arrived in the city and were annoyed that the referee hadn't delayed his decision until about 3 p.m., by which time the condition of the pitch had improved significantly. The game was then due to be played on the Sunday afternoon and concerns were expressed that the Scarlets would not be able to persuade their supporters to repeat the journey, along the M4. Fortunately those fears proved to be unfounded as the Recreation Ground, for the second time in two days, was a sea of scarlet, thanks mainly to the generosity of Huw Evans, the Club Chairman, who had contributed £5,000 to pay for the cost of the buses needed to transport the supporters back to Bath on the Sunday. Huw had been Chairman for two years and had put hundreds of thousands of pounds in the club coffers each year. At the time he was Chairman of a very successful computer software company called Malborough Stirling. Years ago he played for the Swansea Rugby Club second team while his brother, Morrie, was one of the St. Helens favourites.

We played well against Bath, especially the pack, winning 27–10, with Stephen Jones, for the second successive game in the Heineken Cup, being responsible for all the Llanelli points. The victory, which allowed us to proceed to the semi-final stage, was apparently worth £250,000 to the Llanelli club at the time, with the players also receiving a welcome bonus. I did not, however, take part in the celebrations that followed the game. A few weeks previously we had gone, as a family, to north Wales in order to celebrate the New Year. While we were there we were told that Susan, Tina's mother, who had suffered from back pains for some time, had been admitted to hospital. Shortly afterwards we were shocked to learn that cancer had spread through her body. A little later on, when I was on my way to Llanfechell in Anglesey, to open an extension to the village school, I was told that Susan was critically ill so I returned home immediately. Within a week or so, as I came off the field at the end of the Bath game, I was told that she had passed away, at the age of 55, after spending just one month in hospital. As a family we felt devastated and shocked that it had happened in such a short space of time. We were very close to Susan and, since Tina worked in the Neath area, she was able to leave Billy (before he started full-time in school), and then Harry, with her every day. Harry was just two years old when she died. Losing her was indeed a heavy blow for us.

The start of the 2002 Six Nations Campaign was a disaster for Wales, losing 10–54 to Ireland in Dublin. Following that match Graham Henry resigned as the national coach, to be replaced for the rest of the Championship by Steve Hansen, who was subsequently appointed to that position in April. Once again, following that particular game, we players suffered the unpleasant experience of being booed by our own supporters, this time at the airport on our arrival home, when we were also serenaded with the refrain *"We've got the worst team in the land!"*

Personally I felt that I was no closer to Graham, when he left, than when he started as coach. Other players, however, like Rob Howley and Neil Jenkins, really appreciated his contribution and were quite close to him. Neil would say, for example, that it was Graham who was responsible for his success as an outside half since he gave him more freedom to play his own game.

As far as the team was concerned Graham also introduced a sophisticated system to open play, namely the 'pod' pattern. It was also applied to the lineout, where specific clusters of three or four players were responsible for winning the ball, with each pod containing a particular jumper and several lifters.

The pod system in open play could appear complicated. This, roughly, is how it worked: in order to avoid forwards having to run across field to every ruck or maul following a scrum or lineout there would be specific clusters of players who would be expected to do this at particular stages. For example, after a scrum, the open-side flanker would be expected to reach the ball first and then feed the scrum-half or the outside-half. Then numbers 4,5,6 and 8, namely the first pod, would receive the ball and continue in the same direction. As that pod would be stopped and the ball transferred to the scrum-half, numbers 1,2 and 3 would form a second pod to receive the ball from him. That pod would then proceed in the same direction or perhaps in a different direction, the scrum-half or the outside-half making the appropriate call. Then the pattern would be repeated for possibly five rucks or mauls. Those pods would also be used in exactly the same way throughout the game following scrums.

The pod would again be used following lineouts but not in quite the same way, since the pattern can change slightly from lineout to lineout. For example it's possible that, at a particular lineout, a pod made up of numbers 3, 5 and 6 would be responsible for winning the ball. So when number 7 would get to the breakdown first, numbers 1, 4 and 8 would form the first pod in open play to receive the ball, which would then be transferred to the scrum-half, perhaps, when that pod is stopped. The scrum-half would then feed a second pod, containing numbers 3, 5 and 6, and so on. Of course the actual make-up of the first pod, following a lineout, would depend on where exactly the ball was thrown in that particular lineout and on which pod was responsible for winning it.

There were definite advantages to the pod system but it did require the team to play in a slightly robotic fashion, which prevented players from responding spontaneously to what they saw in front of them. Steve Hansen also employed the pod system but usually only for the first two phases following the set piece. At that point the players were expected to look up, take stock of the possibilities and call a move. In addition, if someone made a break, Steve would emphasise the importance to that player of having available options so that he wouldn't 'die' with the ball.

The way that Graham Henry inspired Wales to achieve ten successive victories at the beginning of his period as coach gave the game in Wales an important boost at the time. But I don't think that he appreciated, when he first arrived, how passionate the Welsh people are about rugby nor how physical Six Nations rugby could be. He hadn't realised either that certain aspects of the game were refereed differently here compared to the Southern Hemisphere. I believe Steve Hansen, too, was just as surprised. In any event I think both of them enjoyed their time in Wales and that they, and rugby in New Zealand, benefited from their experience as coaches here.

Following Graham's resignation we lost every game but one that season, which included another hiding by England, the only win being our encounter with Italy. We finished bottom but one in the Championship table and our record for winning our own lineout ball was worse than that of any other country. I, personally, was very glad that Steve Hansen had taken over, despite the fact that he left me out of the team for the Scotland match. He made a point of explaining to me his reason for this decision, namely that he wanted to see how another hooker, in this case Barry Williams (as it happened, in his last game for Wales), could handle the new tactics.

That was one of his *fortes* as coach, namely his readiness to talk individually with players on a personal level. Although we as forwards were still having a hard time at the lineouts, not having been fully persuaded of the benefits of the new system, we were prepared to admit that it had 'something' to offer. Steve was aware of the situation and was prepared to listen to our reservations. That was another of his qualities – he liked to see players challenging the *status quo*, if they had valid reasons for doing so. He would then initiate deliberations with them but without ever taking offence. At the time he was convinced that the lineout situation was going to improve and was prepared to defend us to the hilt in the face of all the flack that we were getting. He was suspicious of the press and was critical of those former international players who were so ready to find fault with us. He would always impress upon us that it was essential to ignore their comments. To him the wellbeing of the team and the players was all-important and he would do everything possible to protect it.

At the end of April the Scarlets travelled once again to Nottingham to face Leicester in the semi-final of the Heineken Cup. We were quite confident that we could win since we had beaten them at Stradey earlier in the competition. The fact that the final, that year, would be played at the Millennium Stadium was an extra incentive but once again we were thwarted. After a very close encounter, Tim Simpson, in the very last minute, landed a penalty, from two yards inside his own half, which went over via the crossbar. There were suspicions that, before taking the kick, he had moved the ball forward some two yards from the actual mark! It couldn't have been a more painful climax. For us, as a club, there was some consolation in the fact that we won the Welsh-Scottish League later that season by beating Cardiff at the Arms Park, thanks to a last-minute Stephen Jones kick. However, the big prize had eluded us once again.

The national squad was looking forward to touring South Africa and I was pleased to be included because, surprisingly, many of our most experienced players, such as Scott Quinnell and Chris Wyatt, were not selected for the trip. Indeed Steve Hansen had chosen a young, comparatively inexperienced team for the two Test matches. Yet there was now a strong feeling in the party that we were beginning to gel and pull together. The people that Steve had brought in as part of the coaching and management team, such as Andrew Hore, who was in charge of fitness, Scott Johnson, as skills coach, and Alan Phillips, the team manager, were now beginning to exert a positive influence. Despite losing our pre-tour match against the Barbarians in Cardiff by 25–40, we players didn't believe for one moment that we were going to be a push-over for the Springboks, in spite of what the press and the media in general were expecting.

Although we lost the First Test by 34–19, with Dwayne Peel and Michael Owen winning their first caps, we played exceptionally well and for long periods we were the better team. That day Michael Owen became the 1,000[th] player to be capped for Wales and by this time Steve had initiated the custom of denoting on every player's jersey his particular place in the hierarchy of those who had been chosen to play for their country since the very beginning. So each time I took the field '913' would be printed under the three feathers on my jersey, which was my particular number in the Wales hierarchy. Since that day, therefore, Michael Owen's shirt has always borne the number 1,000.

I only have about ten of my jerseys left since I've tended to keep the ones that are of special significance to me, which usually relate to the importance of the games in which they were worn. I also have the shirts of each of the countries that I played against, 14 in all. The practice of having numbers on shirts to denote the place of each player in the rugby hierarchy of Wales was part of Steve's intention to make every one of us aware of the importance of the privilege of being asked to wear our country's jersey. What he wished to convey was, "This is your chance to be in possession of this particular jersey ... look after it and wear it with pride". There was a particular incident during that afternoon which gave me great pleasure and that was Martyn Madden coming on as a replacement to win his first cap. By this time he'd been working very hard on his fitness and thoroughly deserved his chance. There are some people who can fill a room with their presence, and who are a breath of fresh air in any company and Martyn is one of them.

Many expected South Africa, in the Second Test, to avenge with gusto the fact that we ran them so close in Bloemfontein. Indeed they engaged in a lot of ominous media talk, prior to the game, concerning the way they were going to "sort us out". Much was made also of the forthcoming 'battle' between myself and James Dalton, the fiery South African hooker. Generally I have little patience with aggressive comments of that nature; the game of rugby has rules, to which everyone must conform on the field of play and, in my book, threatening to beat up and kick heads is not on. Yet that was the kind of atmosphere the Boks, or certainly the media, were trying to whip up before that Second Test. It had obviously created a climate of fear in some circles since, a few days prior to the match, we players were asked to say a few words about ourselves for a particular television channel. Rupert Moon, who was there to provide assistance with broadcasts from South Africa, had quite a fright when I decided to introduce myself to the camera in Welsh. Even though Rupert is extremely supportive of the Welsh language he was afraid that my Welsh input to the proceedings could stir up even more hostility amongst the Springboks and cause them to think that we were making fun of them!

We produced an even better performance in the Second Test although we lost again, this time by 18–9, after being all-square, at 8–8, with just ten minutes remaining. Indeed we succeeded in keeping the opposition front five on the back foot for most of the game. I was happy with my own performance particularly since we won every lineout on our own throw. Steve was very satisfied with the way we played which confirmed what he'd been preaching for some time, that it was the performance that mattered, not the result. We'd shown that, as a team, we were gradually achieving the goals that he, as coach, had set out for us.

It was generally a very happy tour. I shared a room with Mefin Davies and it was he and I who were usually responsible for the entertainment on the bus. Mefin would tell jokes and I would tell a story. Honest! Steve always thought it important to know as much as possible about his players, what their interests were, what kind of books appealed to them etc. For example if one of us was engrossed in a book in an airport lounge, and he happened to walk past, he would always take hold of that book in order to see exactly what we were reading. He did that with me on one occasion when I was browsing in a book of quotations and short stories that I had been given by my father. It was similar to the *Chicken Soup* series to which Steve Black had introduced me in that bookshop in Manly during the Lions tour. Steve Hansen thought the book was very interesting and that I should read excerpts from it to the boys as we journeyed from place to place in the bus, so that they too could derive some benefit from the material. I subsequently did this and although I was initially concerned as to what kind of reaction I would get from the boys I was surprised to hear a few of them admit that some of the readings had had quite an effect on them!

Like most visitors to Capetown I simply had to go to the top of Table Mountain and also visit Robben Island, where, of course, Nelson Mandela and many other prominent members of the A.N.C., had been imprisoned. I also had a chance to see quite a bit of the surrounding country, since my father-in-law, John, had travelled out and had arranged to visit members of the family who had settled there. We spent a very pleasant day seeing various areas of the Cape in their company.

By the time I had returned home my sabbatical year away from my work as a linesman with SWALEC had come to an end and I'd decided to become a full-time rugby player. I was really enjoying my international career and thought that pursuing it on a part-time basis would be impossible. In addition, the nature of my job had by now changed and I was not familiar with certain aspects, such as the new health and safety requirements. Since a great deal of the work could be quite dangerous, especially if you failed to fully concentrate on the job in hand, much importance was attached to new requirements. But sometimes accidents do happen. For example there was that time when I was relying on a garage roof to hold my weight in order to clip a cable on the wall above it. Without any warning the roof collapsed and I fell clean through, landing on my feet on the garage floor. Luckily I wasn't hurt but Mike Clement, who was on top of a nearby pole, almost fell off it because he was laughing so much at my disappearing act. According to John Jones, another member of the gang, it was very similar to a scene from one of the King Kong films where the gorilla is imprisoned in his cage at the bottom of a boat.

At the beginning of July I returned to Bangor to receive an award, which was very important to me, especially since it was granted by one of the most prestigious institutions in Wales, the University of Wales Bangor. It was indeed a great honour to be back in my home patch to receive an Honorary Fellowship and to share the stage with such famous people as Mark Hughes, the Bishop of Bangor, the scientist Dr. Eirwen Gwynn and the artists Gwilym Pritchard and Claudia Williams, who were all receiving the same award.

Once again I was forced to miss a number of games at the beginning of the new 2002-03 season, because of injury. The bones in the main joints of my big toes had been bothering me for some time and I was only able to continue playing by being given pain-killing injections. That's how I managed to play in Llanelli's opening two games in the Heineken competition that year, against Glasgow and Bourgoin. But I was forced to miss the Welsh team's opening matches against Romania and Fiji that season, both of which Wales won easily. Before the Romania game in Wrexham Steve asked me to present the team jerseys to the lads, which I considered to be quite an honour. Wales won easily that day so I was glad to get my place back for the game against Canada on November 16th. It was another victory for us although the performance left much to be desired.

I shall remember the game for two particular reasons, firstly for the magnificent reception that Scott Quinnell received from the Millennium Stadium crowd as he took the field to represent Wales for the last time after winning 52 caps. He'd suffered from quite a few injuries in recent years so his decision to retire didn't come as a great surprise. His contribution to the national team and to the Lions had been immense and we were certainly going to miss him. The second notable event, perhaps for others more than for myself, was the fact that, in that game, I scored my first, and only, try for Wales. It was just a case of my taking a pass from Stephen Jones near their line and falling over to touch down. I left the ball there and ran back to the centre of the field. Apparently Steve Hansen was amazed that I had marked my first try for my country with such muted celebration. To make matters worse Tina had gone to the toilet at that particular time, so she missed my moment of glory!

Indeed it was so typical of Steve Hansen that he wanted his players to show that they were passionate about their country. He, and Scott Johnson too, sometimes made me feel quite ashamed when I didn't know the answers to questions they would ask me about certain aspects of Welsh culture and history. As I have already mentioned, Steve was the one who first got us to call out our lineout codes in Welsh. He was also very keen for us to sing Welsh songs, especially after a match and that was also particularly true of Gareth Jenkins. It was all part of Steve's philosophy that the more someone gave of himself to a particular cause the greater his desire to see that cause succeeding. In other words he considered that the amount of passion we could bring to the Welsh cause was directly related to the 'Welshness' we conveyed. I remember Graham Henry, on one occasion, bringing in a psychologist to one of our discussion sessions in order to enlighten us concerning the importance of 'goal setting'. Steve was standing at the back listening to the address. He then began to question the psychologist until the poor chap didn't know which way to turn. Two years ago, when I was in the company of a psychologist who was part of the All Blacks contingent in Ireland, I repeated that story. *"Ah yes,"* he replied, *"but Steve is a psychologist in his own right!"*

In the same way he would place great importance on 'values'. I still remember the six values which formed the basis of his gospel: respect, unity, belief, honesty, enjoyment and resilience. We witnessed him putting these principles to the test on several occasions. I remember one incident when we were preparing for an international match and had been asked to stay together at the Vale for the preceding week. One of our wingers decided that he was going to spend one night at home towards the middle of that week and would return the following morning. Unfortunately for him Steve happened to be in the hotel foyer when he walked in at breakfast time, whereupon the errant traveller was asked where he'd been. *"Out to the car to get a CD,"* was the reply. *"Where is it then?"* asked Steve, who'd noticed that the player had arrived empty-handed. *"I couldn't find it,"* the winger answered. *"You haven't been home then?"* enquired Steve who was by now suspicious. *"No!"*

Steve, apparently, asked him three times and got a negative

reply on each occasion. The player went to his room and Steve went out to the car park.

It was a cold morning and frost was plainly to be seen on the windscreens of the cars parked in the car park overnight. As a shrewd ex-policeman he noticed that there was no frost on the winger's car and that the bonnet and exhaust pipe were warm. Steve went up to the miscreant's room and, despite being given three further opportunities to admit that he'd been home, he continued to deny that he'd left the Vale. But he had to go home fairly soon afterwards because Steve threw him out of the squad! It seems that his reason for doing so was that he'd been lied to, not because the player concerned had left the hotel.

Another example of the importance of these values to Steve was his message to every player who turned out for Wales that he was to leave the changing room in the same condition as he found it before the game. He believed in leading by example so he and the rest of the coaching staff, after each international match, would be there in their posh suits clearing any rubbish that littered the changing room. In the same way, during tackling practice, it would not be unusual to see him, covered in mud and wet through, throw himself at the tackle bags to illustrate some point or other, despite not being fit, just in order to show the lads that he was happy to join them in such terrible conditions.

There was one other international match to play in November 2002, against the All Blacks, and we had high hopes of beating them for the first time since 1953. Although we lost 17–43 we could well have won the game. After 79 minutes just one score separated us at 17–22 but the visitors came back very strongly and scored three tries in the final few minutes, one of them, ironically, by Regan King, one of the stars of the Scarlets team in recent years and who won his only All Black cap that afternoon. As a pack we were quite pleased with the way we played particularly since we forced the opposing eight to yield a penalty try towards the end. Yet the All Blacks had demonstrated that we had neither the will nor the durability required to sustain the highest standard up until the final whistle.

Efforts to improve the game in Wales had been rather a hot potato for some weeks. The WRU Chief Executive, David Moffat, had produced a plan that would entail replacing the individual clubs that represented first-class rugby in Wales with four new Regional sides, three of which would be in the south and one in the north. The reasoning behind this was that such a development would lead to playing fewer games, which would be of a higher standard. Naturally this meant that some of our traditional teams would disappear but that in itself was of little importance to David Moffat. In his opinion tradition could be detrimental to development and if rugby was going to flourish in Wales at national level, some radical changes were required. He certainly stirred up a hornets' nest and while some factions supported his ideas, others were fiercely opposed, such as the Llanelli club, for example, who embarked on a vigorous campaign to ensure that it retained its individual status. In my opinion, its record over the years fully merited such consideration. David Moffat's plan was subsequently changed in a number of ways, particularly the intention to create a new regional club in north Wales. I have already explained how I think the game should be developed in that particular area but it's interesting to note that many prominent figures in the world of rugby have urged the Union to prepare plans for creating a regional side in north Wales in due course.

Since my big toes were becoming increasingly painful, Steve Hansen advised me to undergo surgery so that I could be fit for the World Cup. It was good to know that I was being considered for Australia so, at the beginning of 2003, I had an operation to cleanse the big toe joints. As a result I missed all of the Six Nations matches that season, which proved to be a disastrous campaign for Wales. We lost every game, including, for the first time ever, the one against Italy. My only personal contribution was as a pundit during the television coverage by S4C!

Because I hadn't played since January 17th I had to undergo a fitness test before facing Perpignan at Stradey in the quarter-finals of the Heineken Cup. We had high hopes but, once again, they were dashed as we were beaten 19–26. In fact we were up against it from the start when Dafydd Jones, our flanker, got sent off for stamping during the opening period. It was all the more disappointing because it was a game we could have won. I was still troubled by the big toe and Aled Gravell took my place shortly before the end but it had felt good to be back playing again. However, we were still in the Principality Cup competition and we took a lot of pleasure from sweeping Cardiff aside in the semi-final, with our highest score ever against them, 44–10. On then to the final and a telling victory against Newport by 32–9, which gave us the Cup for the twelfth time, a remarkable record.

# CHAPTER 11

# Taking On the World

Let the world know you as you are, not as you think you
should be, because sooner or later, if you are posing, you will
forget the pose, and then who are you?

**Fanny Brice**

IN PREPARATION FOR the World Cup, which was to be held
during the autumn of 2003, Wales arranged to play two
games, against Australia and New Zealand, in June but just
before the team was due to depart for the Southern Hemisphere
the players refused to leave the Vale Hotel until the on-going
dispute with the WRU over financial terms and insurance was
settled. The matter was eventually resolved but the travelling
party was, by that time, very late departing for Heathrow with
the result that we missed our intended flight. Although we
succeeded in getting another flight a little later the change to
our original travelling plans meant that the WRU had to fork
out £150,000 in transfer charges. Some blamed the players
for this 'unnecessary' expense but the Union was also at fault
in that it hadn't foreseen the players' protest. After all, the
media had forewarned them the previous day that trouble
was brewing. That said, I must confess that, for my part, the
main concern was to get to Sydney as soon as possible so that
we could start playing rugby. This was another example of
my aversion to discussions involving money.

The match against Australia proved to be an encouraging
start to the trip, despite the fact that we lost 10–30. It was a hard
game, during which we displayed plenty of fire and tenacity
to give us sufficient encouragement to go to Hamilton for the
encounter with the All Blacks in a very positive mood. We were

welcomed there, in the traditional Maori manner, on a *marae*, which is the spiritual centre of every Maori tribe. Of course two of our coaching team, Steve Hansen and Andrew Hore, as natives of New Zealand, were very familiar with this custom and knew that we, as a party, were required to respond to that welcome in our own tongue. Before leaving Wales Steve had appointed Colin Charvis, Martin Williams, Stephen Jones and myself as joint captains for the trip. The main reason for this arrangement might have been to relieve Colin of some of the pressure he had endured from the media following the team's recent poor performances. Apart from that, I could see no point in the new style of leadership, until I got to that *marae* and Steve asked me to respond to the welcome in Welsh. I can't remember what I said but all I know is that, as far as the eloquence of my presentation was concerned, it was just as well that our Maori friends weren't able to understand!

We weren't, however, aware of any generous spirit on the field when we met the All Blacks shortly afterwards. We were hammered 53–3 and the gulf between the two teams appeared to be huge. My abiding memory was the blow that Colin Charvis received in a tackle by Jerry Collins and Tana Umaga's response as he endeavoured to ensure that Colin hadn't swallowed his tongue. They were so much better than us in many aspects of the game, especially those that called for a combination of speed and power. Yet I felt we were comfortable against them in the tight, until I was forced to leave the field with an injury ten minutes into the second half. They scored six tries in all, one by a young lad called Daniel Carter, who is now considered by many to be the best outside-half in the world. He also converted all six tries and kicked a penalty goal. One of the merits of playing that particular game, notwithstanding the disastrous result, was that it gave us plenty to work on following our return to Wales. Of course, such a defeat was a bitter pill to swallow yet I think Steve looked upon it as another opportunity to ensure that we would be a better team come the World Cup, especially since we were such a young squad.

At the end of that summer four more games were arranged, against Romania, in Wrexham, Ireland in Dublin and then two games in Cardiff, against England and Scotland. I wasn't selected for the first two games since the coaching team wished to see as many new faces as possible before the World Cup. We won comfortably against Romania but suffered another heavy defeat against Ireland. I was back in the team for the England game, when the visitors, to all intents and purposes, fielded their second fifteen against us. Our performance was riddled with errors and we were soundly beaten 9–43, our tenth successive defeat against the main rugby-playing countries.

That result was the worst send-off possible for the forthcoming World Cup and by this time the knives were out for Steve Hansen. But one game remained, against Scotland, before we were to set off for Australia and he was under pressure from many directions to change the team and bring back more experienced campaigners. He resisted that pressure and to everyone's relief we gave an acceptable account of ourselves as we won 23–9. I was told, on good authority, following that match, that the Welsh Rugby Union was all set to sack Steve if we'd have lost against Scotland, despite the fact that the World Cup was just weeks away.

During that game I injured my big toe once again and there was some concern that I wouldn't be fit enough to go to the World Cup. I was getting regular treatment from Carcus, the WRU physiotherapist, and was told that the pain was something that I'd have to deal with and that I should simply 'dig in'. The names of every member of each squad had to be submitted by September 10th and I was given a final fitness test that very day. Fortunately I came through it successfully and so off we went to Lanzarote for a period of intense fitness training under the guidance of Andrew Hore. It proved to be hard and hot work but we had been well prepared for the heat in our training hall at the Vale Hotel. Shortly before leaving Wales the coaching team had introduced a number of giant gas heaters to the practice sessions so that we could simulate the conditions that we could expect to face in Lanzarote and Australia.

Andrew concentrated on the fitness requirements of the individual and formulated exercises that were tailored to each player's specific needs. He would treat senior players, like Gareth Llywellyn and myself, rather differently. He assumed that the intense training that we'd undertaken over the years had given us the required general aerobic fitness, without our having to run and run until we dropped! Instead, in our particular case, he would concentrate on developing explosive speed and power, while combining the need to increase leg-power in the gym with continual sprinting exercises over specific short distances.

Since we'd worked so hard during our stay in Lanzarote the management team thought that we deserved a night out on the town. We enjoyed a couple of hours together before the bus arrived to take us back to our holiday complex accommodation. The usual practice session had been arranged for the same time the following morning but four of the lads were obviously suffering more than the rest of us as a result of the previous evening's activities and were late arriving at the training ground.

To Steve Hansen's way of thinking such behaviour was unforgivable but, since he was such a big advocate of 'the squad' ethos and the collective responsibility of its members to look after each other, he blamed those who'd got to the practice session on time for not ensuring that everyone else was present. He therefore decided to punish those of us who had arrived at the appointed hour and not the latecomers. Consequently we were required to do an additional training session, in intense heat. The punishment imposed upon the four 'miscreants' was to force them to watch us suffer and thereby make them feel guilty! That was an excellent example of Steve's unconventional psychology in action!

In the beginning we stayed at the same hotel in Manly as I did when I was trying to recover from my leg injury during the Lions tour. It held many bitter memories for me but I was determined, this time around, to enjoy every minute of our stay. I was glad of the opportunity to prove to myself that the Lion's tour turned out to be such a disappointment for me, firstly because of the bad luck which came my way and, secondly, because my attitude at the time wasn't sufficiently mature to deal with it. I'd learnt a lot about myself since then, and was hell bent on making sure things would be different this time.

As I have mentioned previously the hotel had a superb location right on the edge of the beach and the first thing we did on our arrival was to rush down to the sea to engage in a little surfing. Unfortunately there's more to that particular activity than most of us had envisaged and only a few of the more skilful ones among us, such as Dwayne Peel, were able to stay on their surf boards for any length of time. However, not all leisure pursuits in Manly were as harmless and I had one of my most exciting experiences ever during our stay there, which was to swim in a huge tank with a number of greynurse-sharks, along with about a dozen of the other lads in the party, all of us being more nervous than we'd ever been on a rugby pitch!

At the start of our trip the Australian media interviewed us individually as they tried to create pen-pictures of all the players who would be taking part in the World Cup. I had answered similar questions on many previous occasions during my career so, by this time, I was trying to think of something more original and witty to say when offering a reply. So when they asked whether there was one particular word, as opposed to any other, which inspired me to make even greater efforts, I answered, tongue-in-cheek, *Sais*, which is the Welsh word for 'an Englishman'. They naturally wished to know the meaning of this word but I declined to translate in case I created a diplomatic incident!

For the most part during our stay we remained in Canberra. As far as I know it was chosen, and wisely so, because there was little to do there and it was possible therefore to concentrate on practice sessions and preparation. Since the HQ of the Australian National Sports Institute was also located in that city it had excellent facilities. Everything that we needed was to be found in the particular centre where we were staying, with the exception of a stadium where we could practice. But we were allowed to use the local Rugby League ground, home of the Canberra Raiders and within easy reach.

The accommodation arrangements there were also excellent. We were staying in flats rather than a hotel, with two players sharing each flat and with three or four flats on each floor, consisting a 'team' of residents. This meant that the squad was divided into four teams. Shane Williams was my partner and, like everyone else, we were responsible for shopping for our own food and cooking our own meals, for washing our own clothes (there was a washing machine there) and so on. In the boys' opinion this was an excellent system since it served to bring a sense of order and organisation to our daily life there. Staying at a hotel can often be a miserable existence that can easily lead to laziness, and in order to instil a greater sense of community one 'team' would sometimes invite another to join them for an evening meal. In addition, about twice a week, the four 'teams' would come together at a local restaurant and there were many to choose from in the vicinity.

Another important aspect of our social life at that time was the choir. In the past, forming a choir from amongst Wales and

Lions players was almost an automatic procedure on tour. Steve Hansen had asked me to get a choir together during our stay in Australia, with particular emphasis to be placed on singing a song in Welsh. His desire to respect that Welsh tradition was, to him, perhaps, an example of maintaining "the values" which, in his view, were so important. I was, therefore, given the responsibility of providing our songsters with the words for our renditions. The process had one great shortcoming. Everyone, including members of the coaching team, was expected to join the choir, even if they possessed a voice that sounded like a croaking raven! In order to enhance the cultural status of the choristers I gave each one a Welsh bardic name, for example Brent Cockbain was to be known as 'Pen pìn' or "Pinhead", and Dwayne Peel as 'Gwddw Hir', or "Dwayne of the Long Neck". We had a number of singsongs during the tour, lasting usually for about half an hour, in various locations such as restaurants, barbecues or rugby clubs to which we'd been invited.

An example of the importance that Steve attached to cultural roots was our visit to the Welsh Society in Manly. Many Welsh people, of course, had emigrated to Manly early in the twentieth century to work in the coalmines there. The purpose of our visit was to receive our World Cup caps. Although a player is actually presented with a cap only on the occasion of his first game for his country, everyone who played in the World Cup was awarded a special blue cap. Steve and 'Jonno' were keen for us to get some experience of the traditional culture of Australia and were given a daily history lesson by Jonno, who acted as our tour guide. We were entertained on one occasion by a 'bush poet', after which we were invited to take part in a verse-writing competition. On another occasion Scott gave a talk on the history and culture of the Aborigines. However, one of the most memorable events was our visit to the museum that commemorates the Gallipoli Campaign, to which Australian soldiers made such an essential contribution.

Our first game was against Canada at the Telstra Dome in Melbourne. Most of the preparatory work in Canberra had concentrated on what the coaching team deemed to be our weaknesses, for example the patterns we adopted as a team following scrums and lineouts and our play at the break-down area, in particular how many players we should commit to that aspect on specific occasions.

Steve had also asked a coach from New Zealand, Mike Cron, to join us shortly before the World Cup and work on our scrum. Over the years forwards coaches had analysed in detail the requirements and possibilities of the lineout, but Mike was the first person that we had encountered who had done similar work on the scrum. He was a former member of the front row union himself and believed, as he would remind Steve Hansen often, that it was possible for a coach to teach 95 per cent of that which is important in a scrum but that it needed someone who had actually played there to apply the additional 5 per cent. Mike's main message was how to ensure that forwards adopted the most efficient body angles when packing down. He would also stress that the front row should never go down in isolation, but wait until the other five pack members were joined to them so that they were in the strongest position possible to exert pressure when engaging with the opposing pack. Mike didn't like using a scrummaging machine much in training as he considered it to be too static a method for teaching scrummaging skills and didn't adequately reflect the various scenarios that would occur in a scrum during a game. He preferred, during training sessions, to split the pack and have them scrummage against each other, as front rows, front fives or sometimes four against four, with special emphasis on putting the tight-head prop, who is the cornerstone of the scrum of course, under pressure in order to ascertain his weaknesses.

The game against Canada was quite easy and we scored five

tries, to win by 41–10, with Iestyn Harris kicking five conversions and two penalties. The highlight for me was, as I mentioned earlier, that opportunity early on to flatten Rod Snow, the Gwent Dragons and former Newport prop, with a crunching tackle. In our practice sessions prior to the game Clive Griffiths, our defence coach, would offer additional tackling practice to those who wanted it. Since it was one of the facets of the game I enjoyed, I would spend quite a lot of time working on tackling techniques and it paid off handsomely when I hit Rod Snow. It wasn't hard for me to time the tackle as he ran straight at me, trying to run through me and, without wishing to appear callous, seeing him at my feet was a source of inspiration for me for the rest of the match. I was replaced with twenty minutes remaining, but I had been told in advance by Steve that he was going to give Huw Bennet a run-out during the early stages of the competition.

We returned to Canberra from Melbourne to prepare for the game against Tonga. During past periods of inactivity at the Vale Steve Hansen had brought in an IT expert so that we could familiarise ourselves with that particular technology. The next step then was to have us use laptops to analyse different aspects of our game. In Canberra there was one computer for every two squad members and we were expected as individuals to study different aspects of our play in our most recent matches. I would be able to see, for example, whether I was in the right place, running at the right angle when attacking and whether I looked comfortable in the role I played in defence. With regards to the set piece I could look at the timing and accuracy of the lineouts and my body position in the scrum.

The coaching team expected each player to do his homework on the laptop. Then Steve would analyse the information he would be given by each individual player and criticise, commend or question each one in turn, as required. Also members of the squad who weren't playing against Canada, for example, were to analyse Tonga's play, noting their strengths and weaknesses. Their brief was to analyse different aspects of the game in order to present a report to the rest of the squad, with the aid of video clips and advice from the coaching team. This exercise would ensure that the team selected to play against Tonga would be that much more aware of what they could expect from the opposition.

I was disappointed that I hadn't been selected to face Tonga, but realised that there were two other hookers who also needed to play. As for the game itself we tended to play to their strengths, despite all our preparatory work. It was consequently a very tense match that we were relieved to win in the end, by 27–20. Some of the lads also carried that tension through to the next game against Italy, perhaps because they were part of the Wales team that was beaten by them, for the first time ever, eighteen months earlier in the Six Nations. There was some bad feeling between the two teams ever since that day. Of course the Italians were absolutely delighted that they had won but they didn't celebrate that fact with the customary joy but rather with derision, contempt and gloating, which left a very bad taste amongst the Wales players at the time.

I hadn't played in that particular match so I didn't have to carry that baggage with me to the game against Italy in Australia. It was a match during which they certainly won more possession than us and we were forced to make twice as many tackles as our opponents before eventually winning by 27–15. But first and foremost we were through to the last eight and the relief was evident throughout the squad. All the hard work that we'd done on fitness, strength and power had paid off and we had perhaps surprised some of our critics who'd predicted that we had no hope of progressing beyond the Pool stage. Yet we still had one more game to play before the quarter final, against the mighty All Blacks. Some were of the opinion that we hadn't done enough in our three opening games to avoid being thrashed by

New Zealand, but we knew otherwise.

There was an excellent spirit in the squad, with confidence at a higher level than it had been for many years. Another method the coaching staff used to help get us in the right frame of mind before each game, was to have famous personalities from the world of sport present us individually with our jerseys and share some of their own experiences. During the World Cup Scott Johnson got Mal Meninga and Andrew Johns, the world-famous Rugby League stars, and Glen McGrath, the renowned cricketer, to perform this task and answer the questions we asked them. Graham Henry had started this custom in Wales, with stars such as Gerald Davies and Ray Gravell being asked to draw upon their experiences to inspire the team.

Sometimes, as was the case before the England game in the quarter-finals in Australia, a person with no connection whatsoever with sport would be asked to address us. On that occasion a senior army officer came to read an address given to a particular group of soldiers by one of their officers during the First World War. The crux of the address was that every soldier was to fight to the death and that if that officer saw any one of them trying to escape he would shoot that soldier himself. That particular message had quite an effect on us players before facing England. In fact when famous ex-players came to address us they really didn't have to say a great deal since we knew that their track record spoke for itself. Nevertheless, inviting someone from outside the world of sport was sometimes a tactic that backfired. One of the most disappointing addresses we experienced was when Rhodri Morgan, the Welsh Assembly First Minister, came to present us with our jerseys. He took it upon himself to offer some advice as he did so, such as telling Gareth Thomas, *"Now don't get isolated"*!

The instructions that we were given by Steve Hansen before going out to face New Zealand were, *"We're through but we must get through this game with our heads held high. Go out there and play rugby, but within reason. Don't do anything stupid!"* There were ten changes from the team that had faced Italy, with Shane Williams being able to play for the first time. Since arriving in Canberra he'd been ill as a result of catching some virus and had been confined to his room for most of the time. But he was really up for this game and from the moment he picked up the ball at the base of a ruck in his own 22 and danced up field the pattern for the rest of the game had been established. The aim was to try and retain possession, to keep the ball in hand and to play creative rugby. That's exactly what happened and every member of the team succeeded in raising his game. To everybody's amazement we were in the lead with only twenty minutes to go but unfortunately ran out of steam by the final whistle and eventually lost 37–53.

The question on everyone's lips now was could we give a similar performance a second time and be a threat to England's hopes. We were certainly more confident going into that game and intended running at them as we did against the All Blacks. Of course we'd spent time analysing their patterns of play but our basic aim was to keep hold of the ball rather than kick it away. Ironically it was only after they had resorted to the telling kicks of their replacement, Mike Catt, that England managed to beat us, by 28–17. Prior to that we had again played thrilling rugby and succeeded in scoring three tries to England's one, yet realising that we should have scored more. Our defence was also excellent and for the second time in the competition we succeeded in making over 170 tackles in a game. However, in the end, England were too strong for us and we were forced to yield a number of penalties, which Johnny Wilkinson kicked so clinically.

We were naturally disappointed that the game had slipped from our grasp and it was obvious that Steve, too, was dismayed.

Yet we had, at last, been able to play the type of game that we had been striving for from the outset under Steve and the coaching team. The world had now begun to take notice. It was obvious from the many Welsh supporters whom we met out there that they had been very impressed by our performance. I often think that they would prefer to see us losing while playing the type of rugby that we displayed against New Zealand and England than winning while performing poorly and without conviction. I never make a point of reading press reports of games, particularly ones in which I have played. But it was obvious, after speaking with the media rugby correspondents when they conducted interviews with us following the game that the Press, without exception, were full of praise for the thrilling manner in which we had played during that World Cup.

The morning after the England game the usual riotous Kangaroo Court was held. It is a regular occurrence on tours, when players have to perform all kinds of ludicrous penalties for 'crimes' supposedly committed by them during the trip. I was appointed the Judge and I made sure that every player was guilty of some misdemeanour. Yet the boys had been much kinder towards me since they had chosen me as Player of the Week during one of the weeks on tour, an award which carried with it one of Mal Meninga's shirts as a prize. But our coaching staff voting me the 'Squad Player of the World Cup' was what gave me the greatest pleasure of all. I had four decent games in Australia but it was my efforts off the pitch that earned me the accolade. I knew in myself that I hadn't held anything back, and that I had contributed as much as I could to help keep the team spirit going, as had others. So receiving that honour from Steve Hansen and his team was, for me, the crowning glory of a very satisfying trip, which I had enjoyed more than any other rugby tour that I had undertaken.

# CHAPTER 12

# The Grand Slam

It is amazing what you can accomplish if you do not care who gets the credit.

**Harry S Truman**

I WATCHED THE rest of the World Cup from the sofa, in Tumble, and the caravan, in Port Eynon. Seeing England win the final was a little unexpected but for me the greatest shock was Australia's victory over New Zealand in the semi-final. I was looking forward to taking a break before returning to play for the Scarlets at the end of November. When that time came I could feel the same urge to resume playing and there was no indication yet that I was getting too old!

We did exceptionally well in the Heineken Cup pool games, finishing top of our group. We had two good wins against Northampton and I took a lot of pleasure from being named 'Man of the Match' at Franklin Gardens, where the score was 9–18. That gave me quite a kick since the opposing hooker was Steve Thompson, who'd helped England become World Champions in Australia a few months earlier. By putting a lot of pressure on Thompson, and with the help of a special effort from the props, John Davies and Iestyn Thomas, we succeeded in keeping the Northampton pack on the back foot and forcing them to shoot up in the scrum. But the lasting memory from that game for most people was the fantastic try scored by Barry Davies from his own half.

Yet losing 10–27 against Biarritz at Stradey, in front of twelve thousand supporters, in the next round, was a huge disappointment. On the day we were well beaten by a much better team. What made it a bitter pill to swallow was the fact that some of us senior players knew that it had probably been our best, and possibly our last opportunity, to make an impression in the Heineken Cup. Yet there was some comfort to be drawn from winning the Celtic League that season despite the fact that many of the national squad members in the Llanelli side had been unable to play for the club for some months at the start of the season.

Much was expected of Wales in the Six Nations Championship in 2004 but we finished fourth, after beating Scotland and Italy and losing to the other three countries. I hadn't been able to play against Scotland because of a back injury that I'd sustained during training. I also had to withdraw from the team to play France because of tonsillitis, which seemed such an innocuous complaint but one that left me feeling as weak as a kitten. The final game of that season against Italy was important mainly because it was Steve Hansen's last match as National Coach. We gave an impressive performance to win 44–10 and scored six tries. For us, the players, it was important that we gave Steve a positive and memorable send off. What impressed me most was the way in which the crowd at the Millennium Stadium that day seemed to acknowledge Steve's endeavours during his period in charge, despite the fact that the results of the national team under his direction had been quite disappointing. The supporters appeared to realise that he'd kick-started a new, exciting period and their applause when they bade him farewell was a genuine expression of their thanks. Steve doesn't do emotion but that day, when he stepped on to the field to wave his goodbyes, he confessed that he had shed a few tears.

I have no doubts that Steve is one of the best coaches that I've had the pleasure of playing under. Others, like Gareth Thomas, Gethin Jenkins, Martyn Williams and Colin Charvis have also admitted that he was responsible for opening their eyes at the highest level. He certainly arrived in Wales at the right time as far as my career was concerned, at a point when I had matured as a person and as a player, and we hit it off from day one. He was a 'new ideas' man and wanted the players to have open minds with regard to trying out new things to see if they would work. I appreciated that kind of thinking and was prepared to give it a go. For example, even though we forwards didn't take to his new system at the lineout for some time, it paid off in the end. Yet he was prepared to admit, sometimes, that his ideas were not going to work. For example he was keen to try a system whereby three forwards would be responsible for lifting the jumper at a lineout. We tried it out but it didn't work. But Steve always appreciated our willingness to 'give it a go' and even if we weren't in agreement with him on certain matters he was always prepared to listen to our reasons.

He would also look to challenge you away from the rugby field, when you'd have to endure his dry humour, and we'd have a lot of fun winding each other up. He always saw me as a fiery nationalist and having read about the exploits of Meibion Glyndŵr (an anonymous group who conducted a campaign of burning second homes in rural Wales) he took great pleasure in provoking, for example, Garan Evans and myself that we probably spent our leisure time planning such actions in West Wales. Indeed he would often refer to us as the "cottage burners"! All the players enjoyed the banter with him, without taking things too personally. Before leaving he wrote to me expressing his thanks for my contribution and support during his period with the national squad, and added that he thought I should consider coaching on my retirement as a player!

During May Mike Ruddock was appointed to succeed Steve Hansen as National Coach, much to the surprise of myself and very many others, who were expecting the post to be offered to Gareth Jenkins. Yet in the beginning I hadn't realised how shabbily Gareth had been treated. Of course, as someone who had benefited from his experience and talent for years at Stradey, I felt very disappointed for him. The news that Mike Ruddock would now be in charge certainly didn't inspire me, mainly because of the relationship that I had with him in the past. But I knew that a lot of things had changed, including my attitude, since the time he last coached me.

However, months went by before I was able to rejoin the Wales squad. During a pre-season weightlifting session with the Scarlets, I was doing step-ups on to a bench whilst holding dumb-bells in each hand. To my surprise I discovered that my right hand had very little grip and that I was unable to hold on to the dumb-bell for the duration of the exercise. As a result, I went for some tests and scans to try and find out what was wrong and discovered that there was a problem with one of the discs in my neck. I was advised by the doctors concerned to take a complete rest for three months, at the end of which the condition would have hopefully improved. During that period I continued to keep fit by rowing, swimming and cycling but I wasn't allowed to do any exercises that involved lifting anything above the shoulders, to avoid any compression of the spine.

Mike Ruddock took Wales on a tour of Argentina and South Africa during the summer and then they played four games during November, with victories against Romania and Japan and narrow losses against South Africa and New Zealand. During this period I had started to coach the Scarlets under 18s youth team, and it was during one of their regional matches that I bumped into Mike for the first time. He, of course, knew about my injury but, since I hadn't as yet been able to rejoin the Wales squad, he greeted me, tongue-in-cheek, with the words, *"What's the matter, don't you want to work with me any more?"*

Mike liked to stick with the same squad once he had chosen it, so I was half-expecting to lose my place for the 2005 Six Nations

*At Stradey Park, ready for action!*

*The front row against Bath, 2002.*

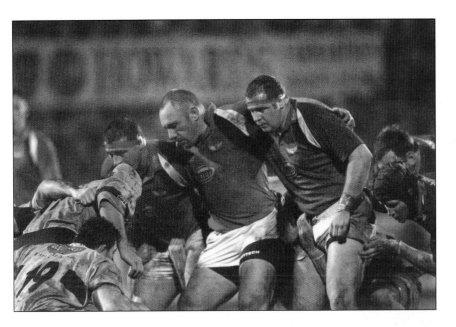

*Chris and me receiving our caps and Stephen passing another record (below).*

*Celebrating the victory against France in Paris, 2001.*

*The Lions, 2001.*

*Above: Harry and me enjoying a little game at Tylney Hall before I leave for Australia.*
*Below: the try that Tina didn't see!*

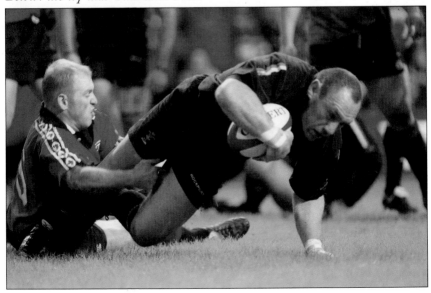

*The Welsh Squad for the 2003 World Cup.*

*Five of us reading the paper — two to hold it, one to turn the page, one to point finger, and one to read out loud!*

*The choir practicing!*

*Making use of the water taxis on one of our days off.*

*Playing hide and seek with the shark!*

## The men you wouldn't want to meet in rugby's dark alley

# HARD
# Bastards...

Take that: Martin Johnson is on the receiving end of Corne Krige's elbow, while Wales feel the force of a Danny Grewcock charge

EVEN rugby's keenest fans admit it is no game for the faint-hearted.

Where teams in other sports have at least one player you would not want to meet in a dark alley, rugby sides invariably have eight. They're known as the pack, those broken-nosed, cauliflower-eared forwards for whom rucking and mauling have become not so much a question of sport as a way of life.

So with the World Cup's appropriately-named 'knockout' phase approaching, DANIEL KING picks out the men who will surely have you hiding behind the sofa as they pursue rugby's ultimate prize.

| NAME | Corne Krige |
|---|---|
| TEAM | South Africa |
| POSITION | Flanker |
| AGE | 28 |
| HEIGHT | 6ft 3in |
| WEIGHT | 15st 10lb |

WHEN Krige called Martin Johnson 'one of the dirtiest captains in world rugby', pots everywhere felt fully entitled to tell some kettles just how black they were. Whatever Johnson's transgressions, at least he roughs up only the opposition. Among a litany of offences during last November's Test at Twickenham, Krige punched his own player, Andre Pretorius, when a forearm smash glanced off England scrum-half Matt Dawson. If not a rugby player, Krige would have been a professional big game hunter.

| NAME | Serge Betsen |
|---|---|
| TEAM | France |
| POSITION | Flanker |
| AGE | 29 |
| HEIGHT | 6ft |
| WEIGHT | 14st 10lb |

HIS countrymen call him 'Les Secateurs' and not because Betsen likes to spend quality time in his garden. The most annoying thing about the way the Cameroon-born star bullied and battered England's golden boy stand-off, Jonny Wilkinson, in Paris last year was that it was entirely legal. Wilkinson was more elusive when the old enemies clashed this year but Betsen had his fun against Scotland, managing to flatten scrum-half Mike Blair with one flying tackle.

| NAME | George Smith |
|---|---|
| TEAM | Australia |
| POSITION | Flanker |
| AGE | 23 |
| HEIGHT | 6ft 11in |
| WEIGHT | 15st 6lb |

HIS dreadlocks make him look like the archetypal surf dude but the only wipeouts involve his opponents. Smith's mission statement of creating 'havoc on the paddock' apparently extends off the pitch, where he has been charged with two counts of assault after an incident outside a nightclub in March. Friends say the voracious and mobile forward is as much a freak of nature as giant All Black Jonah Lomu; opposing half-backs just say: 'Ouch.'

| NAME | Danny Grewcock |
|---|---|
| TEAM | England |
| POSITION | Lock |
| AGE | 30 |
| HEIGHT | 6ft 6in |
| WEIGHT | 17st 7lb |

WITH a name like that, you have to learn to fight and 'Robolock', one of only three men ever sent off while playing for England, certainly did. He's been in scuffles on a regular basis since seeing red against New Zealand five years ago. England colleagues aren't safe either. In June he was sent off in the Parker Pen final for punching Lawrence Dallaglio.

| NAME | Jerry Collins |
|---|---|
| TEAM | New Zealand |
| POSITION | No 6 or Flanker |
| AGE | 22 |
| HEIGHT | 6ft 3in |
| WEIGHT | 16st 3lb |

WALES captain Colin Charvis has a hard-nut reputation of his own, so meet the man whose awesome, head-on tackle left Charvis unconscious with whiplash injuries in June. Even shattered limbs don't stop Samoan-born Collins for long. He once played with a rod supporting a broken leg and, after surgery to remove it, went back to his old job as a binman in Wellington.

| NAME | Robin McBryde |
|---|---|
| TEAM | Wales |
| POSITION | Hooker |
| AGE | 33 |
| HEIGHT | 5ft 11in |
| WEIGHT | 16st 7lb |

MUCH as he likes to play it down, McBryde was once Wales's Strongest Man and it's not just the druids at the Eisteddfod who have felt the force. He has an intimidating physique — built up during years working as a lineman for electricity company Western Power — and a face to match. McBryde is also as hard as nails. Two years ago in Australia he ignored the pain of a blood clot in his right thigh and two tears in the muscle to play for the Lions.

*Surprising how some people see me!*

*Trying to avoid the tackle against Argentina.*

*Breaking through against Italy.*

*Me and the boys with the cup after winning the Championship.*

*Andrew Hore, the Welsh Fitness Coach.*

*Steve Hansen applauding the crowd at this last game as Welsh coach.*

*Scott Johnson who gave me the opportunity to coach the forwards in 2006.*

*With some of the Llan-non schoolchildren after my testimonial match.*

*The fashion show at Tumble hall.*

*Gladys Knight performing for one night only, to raise money for the Tsunami appeal.*

*In Stradey with the boys from Llanfi', including Delme Thomas, a rugby legend*

*Neil Jenkins and me chatting during training in Argentina.*

*Discussing with Duncan Jones, the Welsh captain on the Argentinian trip.*

*Backstage with my father (above),*
*and with Ieuan, Clive and Grav in our robes.*

Championship. When it was announced, I was very pleased that I'd been included in the squad. The first game was against England at the Millennium Stadium on February 5th. We hadn't beaten England at Cardiff for twelve years and the atmosphere was electric throughout the game. The occasion will, of course, be remembered as Gavin Henson's day, who was back in the team after an absence of two years and keen to prove a point. The lads played exceptionally well and won 11–9 after a very tense game. I was battling with my own personal tension as I sat on the bench throughout the game. I was desperate to get onto the field but although Mike Ruddock used five replacements, Ceri Sweeney and I were the ones that didn't have to get up off our backsides. I can't deny that I began to wonder whether I was going to have to suffer, all over again, the misery of sitting on the bench time after time under Mike, for that had been my fate at Swansea all those years ago, and also with Wales. During the final minutes of the game, I was more than aware that Tina and my parents, who were at the match, would have also been sharing my frustrations. As the final whistle blew I knew that they would be looking down from the stand and beginning to think that the dark days were back.

Although I was proud of the performance in that opening game I must confess that I felt quite downhearted that I hadn't been able to contribute at all. This might appear selfish to some, yet I think that it's a perfectly natural reaction and that there must be something wrong with a player who would be quite content to settle for sitting on the bench. During the Italy game, I found myself in the same position, and I spent some time considering my future under Mike Ruddock and asking myself whether I should pack it all in if I wasn't given a chance to take the field there in Rome. I would be happy enough if I got an opportunity to come on as a replacement and make some kind of contribution, and eventually it did happen. After 66 minutes, with Wales playing some thrilling rugby, I came off the bench in place of Mefin, one of seven replacements used by Mike that afternoon. Some of us may not have been on for that long but at least it made us feel a part of it all and kept us from feeling too disappointed.

Again, I was only on the field for fifteen minutes against France in Paris but there's no doubt in my mind that it was one of the most rewarding periods that I'd ever experienced on a rugby field. Both teams had won their first two games in the Championship so the game was expected to be a close one. France came out of the blocks on fire and looked as if they were going to sweep us aside completely but as a result of some solid defensive work and good discipline (we only gave six penalties away throughout the whole match) we were still in contention at half-time with France leading by 15–6. The changing room was relatively quiet during half-time, with no fiery speeches nor any plans to make changes to the team (apart from the fact that Rhys Williams was going to come on instead of Gareth Thomas, who had broken his thumb in five places). We then went back on to the field and raised our game immediately, with Martyn Williams leading the way with two tries. We scored 18 points during that second half, with France scoring just three, and we won eventually by 24–18. But for the last ten minutes our backs were right up against the wall. I've read about players saying that, during a specific period in some games, even though being under great deal of pressure, everything appears to happen in slow motion as it were. I had that feeling too. When I took the field I already knew the advice I was going to give Sid (Robert Sidoli), having had the advantage of watching things from the sidelines.

I took a blow to the knee immediately after coming onto the field so getting the physio to take a look at it was an ideal opportunity to get the pack around and give the boys a breather to enable them to re-focus. John Yapp had also come on to the field shortly after me and we'd hardly any time to adjust to the pace of the game before having to try and prevent the French pack from pushing us over with a series of 5-metre scrums. We held our own without capitulating, although quite a few scrums went to ground. Many of the team and our supporters were afraid that the referee, Paul Honiss, was going to award a penalty try against us but I was quite confident that he could see that the French pack had no momentum at all in the scrums. That is, they weren't able to make us go backwards, so we obviously had no reason to take the scrum down. Hearing the final whistle was a huge relief as we realised that we had not only achieved a remarkable victory but that we had done so in style.

Paris was awash with Welsh celebration that night, but not, unfortunately, for me. The injury that I received to my leg was quite painful after an hour or so and, since we were due to play Scotland in two weeks time, I knew that I would have to take care if I was going to make a contribution to that game. It is, of course, always important not to take alcohol after receiving an injury, so immediately after the official post-match dinner I went back to my room, packed the knee with ice and kept it elevated. So I didn't get a chance to celebrate, although I was warmly invited to do so by Stephen Jones and Dwayne Peel when they called by my room – at three o'clock in the morning!

The injury had improved sufficiently to permit me to take my place once again on the bench for the Scotland game. The team was now full of confidence and, apart from winning three successive games with flair and style, we knew too well that Scotland were going through a bad patch. At Murrayfield we carried on where we'd left off in Paris and at half-time we were 38–3 ahead. Scotland then came back strongly, as always happens when a team is behind by such a margin early on, and scored three tries whilst making us defend doggedly during the final quarter. I went on as replacement three minutes into the second half when Scotland were fighting back, and enjoyed playing my part in a very exciting encounter. The ball was in play for a total of 43 minutes, which was a record for a championship match and reflected the type of game that it was. Yet one thing worried me: during the match I began to feel pains in my neck, and down my right arm, a problem which in due course was responsible for bringing my career to a close.

One game remained before we could claim the Grand Slam and the expectations of the Welsh people were higher than they'd been for many years. We hadn't beaten Ireland in Cardiff since 1983 and they too had a chance of becoming champions if they won by thirteen points or more. The stage was therefore set for a massive encounter. As players we had tried to ensure a fairly low-key atmosphere at the Vale during the week leading up to the game. Of course we couldn't escape the clamour for news and interviews by the press and the media but in general the players managed to stay cool throughout.

I was obviously disappointed again that I wasn't in the starting line-up, but I also recognised that the coaches weren't going to change a winning formula. The only time I discussed my feelings during the championship was with Scott Johnson, when I confessed to feeling rather frustrated about it. His reply was, *"It's not just about you, mate, it's about the team!"* and I had to accept that. Decisions are hard to take sometimes, and players react in different ways. I have experienced that feeling more than I'd have liked to, but one thing I realised is that there is nothing anyone can say or do to make you feel any better; you just have to get on with it.

It was difficult not to feel the fever-pitch atmosphere during the coach journey through Cardiff to the Stadium and we were all desperate to get to the changing room. But on the stairs, on the way there, we came face to face with an emotional 'Gravs', who squeezed the life out of every one of us with his embrace! It was enough to get all the players worked up before entering the changing room. Personally I like to concentrate quietly on the eighty minutes ahead without feeling particularly nervous or having a need to rely on any particular routine or superstition. The same couldn't be said for some, such as Robert Sidoli, who folds each article of clothing meticulously in his bag before thinking of getting prepared for the game ahead. But nothing makes him flustered and having such a calm attitude on such an occasion must be very rewarding.

Although we didn't have the freedom to play with the same flair as we did against Italy and Scotland our performance against the Irish was very efficient, particularly in the light of all the pressure on us to win. And that's what we did, and fairly comfortably, by 32–20, with Ireland playing catch-up throughout the game. Once again I was longing to get on to the pitch, perhaps more so in this game than in any other during the season, particularly as Billy and Harry were there to see it. I was relieved, therefore, to get on for them, more than for myself. It was a great feeling to be part of the celebrations at the end, particularly for those of us who had been through some tough times with the Welsh team over the years. Winning the Grand Slam against Ireland was even sweeter in the light of the fact that Welsh supporters out in Dublin had booed us a few years previously. Yet, despite the thrill I felt when the referee blew the final whistle, for me it wasn't quite up there with the exhilaration that accompanied the victory in Paris.

The celebrations continued in the Stadium for ages. The families of all the players were invited to join them in the changing room and everyone there had an opportunity to have their photograph taken with the Six Nations Championship Trophy. It was obvious from the response of the crowd, as the team bus took us to the post-match dinner at the Hilton Hotel, that the celebrations would last for days! Indeed some were still at it when a few players went walkabout through the streets of Cardiff the following morning. People stopped to congratulate us every step of the way and that remained the case wherever one went in Wales for weeks afterwards.

In addition to winning the Grand Slam what gave particular pleasure was the manner in which it was achieved. Every player had the confidence to play the ball from anywhere on the field. 'We were all singing from the same hymn sheet' as the saying goes, and each individual was prepared to take responsibility for any decision he made. In particular, the skills coaching that we'd been given as forwards on our ball-handling and running angles had paid off handsomely. It was a pleasure to be part of it.

Unfortunately the Scarlets had little to celebrate that season. The performances in the Heineken Cup were disappointing and we failed to progress further than the pool games. Similarly we failed to make an impression on the Celtic League and finished fifth, with the Ospreys being crowned champions.

But there was another reason why 2005 was a special year for me. The Llanelli Scarlets Rugby Club were kind enough to make it my benefit year, after I'd been at Stradey for ten years. In addition the club earmarked our game against Worcester, during August 2005, as a testimonial match for me. That meant having all the club facilities on the day at my disposal, including the gate receipts. Some would argue that, in an era when rugby players are well paid, benefit years no longer have their place, and I can appreciate that point of view. Yet getting paid and being appreciated are two entirely different matters and a benefit gives supporters and the club an opportunity to demonstrate that a particular player's contribution, and his loyalty to that club, has been appreciated. I must confess that I didn't feel comfortable at the beginning with doing the rounds to ask people for their support, but the appreciation that I experienced during that year was amazing. It also gave me an opportunity to express my gratitude to a number of friends for their constant support over the years.

The first thing that had to be done was to organise a Benefit Committee and in that respect everything was placed in the capable hands of Rupert Moon. He himself had already received a benefit year and was able, as a result, to advise as to what kind of events we should arrange. The Chairman of the Benefit Committee was the former High Sheriff of Glamorgan, John Maclean, who took charge of the various meetings and was responsible for opening many of the events with a word of welcome.

Since north Wales had played such a significant part in my upbringing and my career we had to have a secretary for the activities to be held there. In that respect my father agreed to undertake that thankless task and he did a magnificent job. Those who performed that duty brilliantly in south Wales were Tony Jones, David Inkin, Bowen Stevens, David Thomas and Dawn Jenkins, with excellent assistance provided by Dawn's whole family, particularly her husband, Kevin. Unfortunately Bowen passed away during the benefit year, which was a huge loss to everyone in the Llanelli club, particularly the players, since he was quite a character and did such a lot, without a second thought, to help others. Of course, the most important person on any benefit committee is the Treasurer and in my case I was lucky to be able to draw on the services of Colin Stroud, who also looked after the financial affairs of Llanelli Rugby Club.

We held many benefit dinners throughout the country, with a number of stars from the world of rugby as guest speakers, such as Clive Rowlands, Derek Quinnell, Ray Gravell and others too, for example Alun Wyn Bevan and Ifan 'JCB', and not least Judge Mike Farmer who displayed his splendid talent for oratory at the first dinner held at the hall in Tumble.

During the year the support, at a variety of events the length and breadth of Wales, was fantastic. Many of them had to be organised around my rugby-playing commitments of course. However, what proved to be a blessing in disguise that year was the fact that I was forced to miss a number of games because of injury, over a lengthy period, which enabled me to take a more prominent part in the benefit activities. I was amazed at the variety of events that had been organised, ranging from a garden party at John Maclean's house, to golf days and a cricket match, from a night of traditional singing and feasting to a fashion show, mainly organised by Tina, where the Scarlets players, including yours truly, did a Full Monty! On one occasion Salesi Finau even managed to get the Tonga players from various clubs in Wales to come together and sing for us. Indeed we were provided with first-class entertainment at the various locations, by a variety of artists of all ages, not least the pupils of Llan-non Primary School.

Perhaps the most unlikely venue for an event associated with Robin McBryde was the special dinner at the House of Lords in London. The reason for this location was that David Thomas had organised a very successful function there during Rupert Moon's benefit year and I must confess that I really enjoyed my night there. Lord Rowlands was the MC as it were, and the highlight for me was the very entertaining address by Mel Thomas, a former teacher from Birmingham. He was so good that he was invited to appear again at the dinner that brought the benefit year to an end, at Gelli Aur. Similarly, the Rev. Roger Hughes, who included a special prayer for me when saying grace at the House of Lords dinner, was also invited back to that final dinner.

At these events everyone did their very best to ensure that the benefit was a success and I hope that they, too, had a ball while doing so. I am extremely grateful to them all for making that year so memorable and enjoyable.

# CHAPTER 13

# Off the Hook

*Be more concerned with your character than your reputation, because your character is what you are, while your reputation is merely what others think you are.*

**John Wooden**

As I MENTIONED earlier, after the France game in 2005 I was troubled with an injury to my knee, but I also began to get shooting pains, like toothache, from my neck down along my right arm. I wasn't able to sit or lie comfortably with the result that I would be awake most of the night. As we were in the middle of the Six Nations at the time, with prospects looking rather special, I decided that I would try to live with the pain and refrain from drawing attention of the medical team to the problem. During the period I was on the field for the Scotland game I went into one scrum and knew at once that there was something wrong. By this time I found it difficult to get my arm to function normally and trying to hold it at an angle to brush my teeth first thing in the morning was a problem. But by the end of the Six Nations Championship we were no longer having strenuous training sessions so it was only during the actual games that my neck came under any great strain and on those occasions I succeeded in living with the pain.

Following the Six Nations, I was back in full training with the Scarlets, in readiness for the match against Glasgow in the Celtic League. During one of the defensive sessions I missed a few tackles as I tried to shield my neck, and I remember at the time asking myself what on earth was I doing. During that match

I took the field long enough for me to know that the time had come for me to go back to see John Martin, the neurosurgeon at Morriston Hospital, whom I had already been consulting. John had in fact spoken to me constantly, making sure that I was aware of what was happening and was always available to answer any questions that I may have had. After the necessary tests it was decided that I would have an operation at the beginning of June, by which time I was desperate for the injection that would render me unconscious since I was in so much pain. It had got so bad that I had only been able to get to sleep for about an hour or two each night, and in the armchair at that.

When John opened up the back of my neck he expected to find that a disc had shifted from its proper place and that he would have to take it out and replace it with a suitable piece of bone. However, he saw that the disc was completely dislodged and pressing on the nerve, so he succeeded in removing it without any difficulty at all, and the offending disc is now in a jar on the mantlepiece! He told me that he was surprised that I had managed to keep going for so long bearing in mind the extent of the injury. I underwent surgery on the Thursday and on the Saturday John took me to his home, from the hospital, so that I could watch the First Test between the Lions and New Zealand.

When I asked John for his views on my prospects as far as my career as a player was concerned he told me that everything depended on my personal feelings. He was of the opinion that if I were to resume playing I would be unlikely to have any further problems with the neck but that I would be sure to suffer sooner, rather than later, after I'd finished playing. I discussed my dilemma with Tina and, although I knew that she'd be happy with whatever decision I would take, I came to the conclusion that the risk was too great. I counted myself extremely lucky to have had a longer career than most and I wanted to be able to enjoy the rest of life pain free. Therefore, during my benefit dinner held at the home of John and Ann Maclean at Gelli Aur near Llandeilo, on August 26th, I announced that I was hanging up my boots.

I realised that I would miss playing very much, along with the camaraderie of the boys and the lifestyle that I had enjoyed over the years. Similarly I wasn't looking forward to breaking my ties with Stradey, where I'd spent ten happy years. But despite having another year left on my contract with the Scarlets and although I knew that, at 35 years of age, I could still compete at the highest level for a little while longer, I had too much to lose.

I'd had a good run, playing 250 games for the Scarlets, representing Wales 37 times and touring with the British Lions – a career that had given me great satisfaction. My announcement had caused quite a stir, both in the press and, judging from the letters and the cards that I received, amongst personal friends and colleagues from the rugby fraternity. I had no idea that the news would cause such a fuss although it was nice to be the subject of so many good wishes.

However, now that I had retired as a professional rugby player, I had no idea as to what I was going to do for a living. But I was certain of one thing nevertheless: I had no desire whatsoever to return to climbing poles in the wind and the rain for the Electricity Board, and according to my former colleagues the industry had changed substantially since my departure.

During my time as a professional player I had completed the WRU Level 3 coaching course and I'd been a part of the coaching team with the Scarlets Under 18 side for the last two years, with some success, since we had recently won the Union's Under 18 Trophy by defeating the Ospreys in the Final at the Millennium Stadium. I also enjoyed taking a few sessions at Tumble Rugby Club while I was recovering from my injury. I knew what I really wanted to do, which was to coach young players and to do so for two reasons. Firstly, I wanted to give back some of the knowledge that I'd acquired as a youngster and which had been so valuable in my case when I was being primed for a career at the highest level. That basic and all-important coaching was, in my case, down mainly to three people – Meic Griffith, Elvie Parry and Denley Isaac. Secondly, young people can take to coaching and advice much more quickly and readily than players who have been following routine patterns for a number of years.

I had been in discussion with the Union concerning my future and had been informed that the Welsh Rugby Union was about to advertise for a forwards-skills coach to work with Academy players. The post, in addition to the new position of a kicking-skills coach, would supplement the three other coaching-skills posts that were already in existence. It sounded like the ideal job in my opinion so I put in an application for it, knowing that I was up against strong opposition. I gave a presentation as to how I thought I could assist Academy forwards, whilst at the same time drawing on my experience with the young Scarlets forwards. I was subsequently offered the job, along with Neil Jenkins who was given the post of kicking-skills coach.

Not long after I started in my new job Alan Phillips, the Wales Team Manager, suggested that there could be an opportunity to join up with the New Zealand squad during their tour to Britain and Ireland that November. Their head coach was Graham Henry, with Steve Hansen and Wayne Smith as his assistants, and Mike Cron responsible for the scrums. So I met Steve and Mike at a hotel in Cardiff when the All Blacks were playing Wales during that tour and discussed with them what I would like to do. I was soon on the plane to Dublin in order to join up with them during their preparations for their game against Ireland, and I remained with them for their sessions prior to the England game.

I spent most of the time on the touchline watching the forwards training, and having discussions with various coaches.

The first session I attended was the debrief of their match against Wales and it was interesting to see things from their perspective. Indeed, the All Blacks players on that tour were such masters of the basic skills that they were able to pay a lot of attention to what many would consider to be minor details. But those are the very details which ultimately make a fairly good team into a very good one.

With regard to the scrum for example, Crono had been coaching in Japan and had been studying the art of Sumo wrestling. He noted that every wrestler, before hurling himself at his opponent in the circle, appeared to establish a solid platform for himself by contracting his toes, so that he had a good grip of the floor beneath him. Then he would suddenly straighten his toes when it was time to surge towards the other wrestler. Many would think that this has no relevance whatsoever to the scrum, but Mike was able to see things from a different perspective and duly introduced such elements into his sessions.

They also attached a lot of importance to the role of the psychologist when dealing with the players, in particular the younger players on tour. The psychologist was part of the coaching team and one of his duties was meeting individually with new players on the tour, discussing with them what they perceived as weaknesses in their game and trying to establish ways of assisting them. This was already an area that I intended to develop with Academy players in Wales and it was good to see that even the mighty All Blacks were willing to draw upon the services of a psychologist as part of a constructive process to improve the achievements of their players.

In many ways there wasn't much difference between the New Zealand squad and the Wales squad under Steve Hansen with regard to their adhering to an agreed set of values, which included not talking to the press or media without the official blessing of the management team – everything had to be kept within the confines of the squad. On the matter of tactics, in order to prepare for the next game, they followed the same pattern as Wales did in the World Cup. Players would be given the responsibility of analysing future opponents in their particular position and then presenting a report to the rest of the squad. There was one other obvious similarity between us as countries: it was essential to beat the English! Following their victory against Ireland the All Blacks stayed in their hotel that Saturday night, rather than celebrate in Dublin, because of the big game against England the following week. So the players, along with friends and family members, congregated in one large room to socialise and sing a few songs to the accompaniment of some four or five guitars.

However, the squad's methods of relaxation weren't always so harmonious. Once a week for an hour their 'Fight Club' would meet at seven o' clock in the morning and I was invited to join them. We worked in pairs, one wearing gloves and the other having pads on each hand, with the roles reversed after a certain amount of time. The purpose of the exercise was, as I saw it, a way to vent the feelings of frustration or aggression that most of us harbour at times, and rugby sessions don't necessarily provide a release for those feelings. The process certainly gave some of the participants quite a buzz, which was fine in the case of those who were used to such sessions. But to a newcomer like me, and having Jerry Collins as a partner, I had to concentrate so much that the 'feel good' factor took a little longer to sink in.

On my return to Wales I presented a report to the other coaches and the management team, detailing my experiences with the All Blacks. One of the things to which I referred was the custom, by members of their coaching staff, when one of them had a grievance, to get together as a group to discuss that particular matter. Everyone present would have his say and the meeting would continue until the complaint had been resolved.

I happened to mention, in passing, that the All Blacks referred to that process as *"going into the red zone"*. Little did I know at the time that, following the resignation of Mike Ruddock a few months later, it would become one of the most frequently heard expressions during the dispute that ensued. In order to explain to the Welsh rugby clubs the Union's standpoint on the matter of Mike Ruddock's resignation the two senior Welsh Rugby Union officials, David Pickering and Steve Lewis, undertook a kind of whistlestop tour of the country. Even the press began to refer to it as *'The Red Zone Road Show'*, and all because of an oblique reference that was made during my report to the Union on the period I spent with the All Blacks!

I gained a lot from that period with the New Zealand team and I was really looking forward to putting new ideas into practice. There were about 80 players in the Academies, divided between the four regional teams, and my job entailed going to see some of the forwards each week to give them specific coaching. I had some frustrations with the way the system worked, as it involved a lot of time travelling and not a lot of time actually coaching, so the process wasn't as productive as it could have been. That system has changed by now, with each region having been designated its own skills coach, which means being able to work with groups as well as individuals on a more regular basis.

I was surprised when Mike Ruddock resigned in February 2006, in the middle of the Six Nations Championship. Before the start of that international season he had met all of us as skills coaches to explain his plan to involve us in the preparations of the national squad. I had quite a few reservations at the outset, mainly because I had been playing alongside them the previous season and felt that it would be a 'teaching your Granny how to suck eggs' scenario. But the feedback that I had was positive and I thoroughly enjoyed it. The way the players responded to me was fantastic which led to making my next decision as a coach a much easier one.

A few days after Mike's resignation I got a phone call from Alan Phillips asking me if I'd be willing to assist Scott Johnson to coach the national team for the three remaining international matches that season. I didn't hesitate for a moment and jumped at the offer. I had a meeting with Scott and was given to understand that he wanted me to prepare the forwards for the three games, with particular regard to the lineout and the scrum.

The players were certainly under a lot of pressure at that particular time and they felt that they were being held responsible by the press for whatever had led to Mike Ruddock's resignation, which had also alienated the Welsh rugby supporters. Personally, I didn't always see eye to eye with Mike on the rugby front but I always respected his views. I received a message from Mike when I was forced to give up playing, thanking me for my contribution to the national squad during his period as coach and I wished him well in the future when I heard of his resignation.

I was quite happy with the way the forwards performed in the remaining three Six Nations games. I felt we were unlucky against Ireland, when we had to contend with losing Stephen Jones early on, and with the unsympathetic interpretations of the referee, which completely undermined some of our tactics. We won enough possession to beat Italy but we gave them too much freedom to put their stamp on the game. In the same way we competed well against France and were unlucky to lose. So we had a disappointing season after the glory of the previous year.

It was a great pleasure to work alongside Scott Johnson and, prior to that period, to have been coached by him. He was a master at developing skills with the backs and then introducing a number of those skills to the forwards. He liked to be one step ahead of the opposition regardless of which move was called. He would relish discussing ideas, particularly if they challenged the run of the mill thinking about the game. I remember spending time discussing the possibility of having the scrum half, as opposed to the hooker, throw the ball into the lineout. Nothing came of the idea back then, but we enjoyed the debate. His hearty humour and genial personality made him very approachable yet he took his work very seriously and in that respect he was one of the most thorough coaches that I have ever worked with. If I had to find fault at all with him it would be concerning his taste in T-shirts!

It came as no surprise that Scott didn't accept the invitation to continue in his position as National Coach. Yet he was loathe to leave Wales and the last meeting between him and the squad was very emotional for many of the players. Scott had overseen their development through an experimental stage and had seen them grow into mature and talented international performers. They were very grateful to him and, like Scott himself, had enjoyed the experience very much.

At the end of the 2006 Six Nations Championship I didn't know exactly what my position was with regard to my future with the Wales squad. I felt that the forwards had performed satisfactorily in that championship and the official statistics showing the amount of ball they had won during those five internationals confirmed that. I very much hoped that I would be allowed to continue and that I could maintain my links with the squad now that I'd had a taste of it. That opportunity came when Gareth Jenkins came down to Stradey one day, at the beginning of May, while I was holding an Academy session there, and asked me to go on the Wales tour to Argentina, a month later.

He didn't need to ask me twice, for two reasons. Firstly I was keen, as I have already stated, to continue with the work I had been doing with the national squad some months earlier. Secondly, I had never been to Argentina and I particularly wanted to visit the Welsh settlement in Patagonia, where one of the two

Test matches would be played, at Puerto Madryn. During the latter part of the nineteenth century many people from Wales had emigrated there and part of their endowment is a vibrant community, where the Welsh language is still spoken alongside the native Spanish tongue.

We were given a fantastic reception by many of the locals from the moment we landed in Trelew (a number of the place names in Patagonia are Welsh). Over 200 of them came there to greet us, many of whom were wearing the red shirt of Wales. Everybody in the squad was amazed at the extent of the welcome. Before proceeding to Puerto Madryn on the Thursday, to prepare for the First Test there on the Sunday, we stayed at Trelew for a couple of days. A night of special celebrations had been arranged for us, with the emphasis on three things: dancing, singing and feasting. Firstly, one of the town's main streets was closed in order to construct a huge barbecue where thirty lambs had been roasted in our honour, before moving on to the Town Hall to engage in some folk dancing. The Welsh speakers in our party were naturally put to sit with some of the local Welsh-speaking people, and it was such an unforgettably nostalgic experience, with most of the squad being astonished and enchanted by the fact that the Welsh language and culture was so alive in such a distant country, amongst a people who, in most cases, had never been to Wales.

While I was in Trelew I got an opportunity to coach at the local Red Dragon Club, in the Gaiman. Their pitch, as was the case with most of the playing fields we visited, was basically a bare patch of land, and explaining tactics by drawing diagrams with twigs in the dust was indeed a strange experience! I issued my instructions to the players in Welsh which one of them then translated into Spanish for the benefit of the rest of the boys although some of the group also spoke Welsh. Mike Phillips and Nicky Robinson had also accepted an invitation to do some coaching while Rowland Phillips, Shane Williams, Nathan Brew and Jamie Robinson, the other Welsh speakers in the party, visited a school, a chapel and a cemetery, all of which were an important part of the Welsh heritage of the region.

During my time as a player with Menai Bridge a young man from Patagonia, by the name of Waldo Williams (who had been named after one of Wales's most famous poets), turned out for us in a seven-a-side competition in Harlech. Unfortunately he wasn't on the field for long that day for I knocked him clean out as we both went to tackle the same opponent during the opening minutes of our first game. The last time I saw him was when he was being carried off the field after that fateful tackle. When I was in the Gaiman I enquired about Waldo and indeed many there knew him, for he was a former player with the Red Dragon Club. The following day who walked into our hotel to look for me but Waldo! He spoke Welsh and it was great to get an opportunity to share some memories with him and to know that he had eventually forgiven me!

At Puerto Madryn we stayed on the sea shore at a hotel with fantastic views – whales were actually swimming in the bay below us when we arrived. It is a place that has special significance for Welsh people since it was here that the first settlers from Wales landed, from their ship *Mimosa*, in 1865. Some of us went to see the memorial that commemorates the occasion and the nearby caves where the settlers sought refuge during the early days. We also tracked down two tea rooms, bearing the names, in Welsh, Cardiff Tea Room and the Red Dragon Tea Room, where we sampled some superb traditional Welsh cakes!

Our squad for the Argentina tour was young and quite inexperienced but they were very enthusiastic and keen to make an impression. There were no fewer than three new caps amongst the forwards in the First Test, which we lost narrowly 25–27. There were weaknesses in our play on occasions, such as an inability to finish moves more clinically as we managed to break their defence on nine occasions, which is a very high figure for an international match, yet not one of those breaks led to a score. As a pack we were aware of Argentina's strengths, particularly setting up driving mauls to get their game going and sapping the strength of the opposition. To counter this threat at the lineout we had four plans of action, two of which were concerned with preventing the opposition from driving through and two others whereby our jumpers would compete for the ball. As a result of these tactics Argentina were forced to play much more of the game further away from the lineout than they would have liked.

We nearly succeeded in winning the First Test, even though we had to play for a long period with just fourteen men, thirteen at one point since both Gavin Thomas and Alix Popham were in the sin bin at the same time for a while. This was a heavy cross for a young team to have to bear, particularly against a team like Argentina playing on their own patch. The effort and application of the Welsh team was huge on a pitch that suited Argentina's style of play, being both short and narrow, and, to make things worse, they were also awarded a try, which in effect should have been disallowed.

So we went into the Second Test in Buenos Aires knowing full well that we should have, and could have, won that first game. But that supreme effort in Puerto Madryn took a lot out of the boys and we were able to hold just three light practice sessions before the match the following Saturday.

The Second Test was different in many ways. In the first instance the ground in Buenos Aires was much bigger which afforded an atmosphere far more worthy of an international match. In addition, Argentina, who were disappointed with their performance in the First Test, raised their game for the second encounter and were much more physical. They were by far the better team and deserved their victory by 45–27. I was quite happy with the performance of the forwards as we again nullified their driving threat and managed to provide a platform from which our backs could play.

As coaches we were pleased to see how much strength in depth there was in the squad, bearing in mind that a number of senior players had been left at home to recover from a long season that followed the Lions tour. Young players such as Ian Evans, Alun Wyn Jones and James Hook, to name but three, benefited from that decision, and it was great to see how much they developed in such a short time. I really enjoyed the experience of coaching the squad and felt that I had got over the awkward feeling of having played alongside many of the senior members just fifteen months earlier. In a way my familiarity with them as a player and then as a coach was a means of ensuring some continuity since all the other coaches, apart from Neil, were new to the national squad. Yet we had a memorable and harmonious trip despite the fact that being with Rowland Phillips for a fortnight made the experiences of those appearing on *I'm a Celebrity, Get Me Out of Here* seem like a doddle!

On my return home from Argentina, I was informed that I was to receive an unexpected honour at the Swansea and District National Eisteddfod in August, namely being accepted as an honorary member of the Gorsedd of Bards. It came as a big surprise since I had never considered myself to be worthy of such recognition. It was an honour that my father, I'm certain, put on a par with, if not above, that of representing your country on the rugby field. The day itself on the National Eisteddfod Field was indeed one to remember and I was so glad that Tina, Billy and Harry, along with my parents, were there to share the occasion with me. I was quite nervous before the ceremony, especially as I got changed into my robe, but Clive Rowlands and Ieuan Evans, who had been similarly honoured in the past, along with Gravs, who had the official role of Keeper of the Sword, were present and ready with their support. In fact I was made to feel very welcome by everybody. For some time previously I had been worried as to what I should wear under my robe, having been told that things can get quite hot under the spotlights above the stage. Although I would spend most of my working week wearing shorts I somehow didn't think that it would be an appropriate form of dress for the occasion – until I saw the Archdruid, Selwyn Iolen, putting on his robe over his own shorts and T-shirt!

# CHAPTER 14

# Total Immersion

*If you can react the same to winning and losing, that is a big accomplishment. That quality is important because it stays with you the rest of your life.*

**Chris Evert**

DURING THE EARLY part of the 2006-7 season, I spent some time at the regions in order to learn as much as possible about the players that were in contention for places in the autumn internationals. The demands on the regional clubs due to the fixture list did have a considerable bearing on the extent of our preparations for the First Test against Australia on November 3rd, so getting an idea of the background they were coming from was important. With many of our players being involved in games up to the preceding weekend, it meant they would not be able to join the squad until the Monday. Normally, before each international we, as coaches and groups of players, would carry out a SWOT (Strengths, Weaknesses, Opportunities and Threats) analysis of the opposition. This would have been based on Australia's most recent Tri Nations games and their tour of the UK the previous year when they were somewhat exposed as a team experiencing many problems, particularly in the scrum. But they now had new coaches (including Scott Johnson), and although to a large extent the same players were still there, they had changed their style and had rebuilt their team ethos. So, bearing this in mind, we decided to focus even more on our own game rather than pay too much attention to the opposition.

Nevertheless we did, of course, target certain areas where we thought we would be able to gain some advantage, such as the scrum, and setting up a few driving mauls to tie in their back row. In view of the limited time available to us as coaches, we had to rely mainly on the policies and patterns that we had introduced on the summer tour to Argentina. There were slight adjustments to our lineout calls and mindset regarding the scrum, but the main focus was on trying to gel everyone together. We had a full squad to choose from following the return of some of our most experienced players who had been rested for the tour to Argentina; we therefore went into the game feeling quietly confident although realising that, ideally, we could have done with a little more time to prepare.

The intensity of the Australian forward play during the early part of the game, both in the tight and at the breakdown, really took us by surprise despite having had a glimpse of it in their game against the Ospreys earlier in the week. Even though we were winning enough possession from the set pieces, they frequently counter-rucked us at the breakdown, with the result that we were often getting poor quality ball from broken play. So, for the first twenty minutes, we were under the cosh. Gradually we fought our way back and did well to go into the changing rooms at half time with just one point separating the two teams.

I didn't have much to say during the break but we did draw attention to a few 'focus' points on the white board at our disposal as coaches. The players, of course, only have a ten-minute respite, the first part of which is taken up with their need of some recovery time and an opportunity to discuss various aspects of the game with each other. While this takes place we as coaches jot down briefly, on the white board, the basic points we need to convey so that the message is clear to every player before they go out for the second half. During play, conveying such messages isn't as straightforward and you have to try and relay them on to the pitch to your key decision makers during a break in play. It's essential therefore that the 'messenger' is sufficiently skilled to be able to pass on the messages of the coaches correctly.

There was an instance, some years ago, during a game between Wales and Ireland, where a breakdown in communications between the Welsh coaching team and their touch-line messenger led to some confusion. The instruction from above was to "Tell Iestyn to attack John Hayes's outside shoulder", whereupon the message was conveyed to Iestyn Harries, our outside-half on the day, and who hadn't had that much experience of playing Union at the time. He ended up in a rather perplexed state, spending quite some time trying to work out how he was going to get an opportunity to do this against the Irish tight-head. The fact that the instruction was intended for another Iestyn, namely Iestyn Thomas our loose-head prop, was lost in translation!

When the final whistle was blown, the team had battled back to gain an honourable 27–27 draw with the Australians, although some of the players were disappointed that we'd failed to secure a win. There were quite a few positives that we took from the Australia game. We'd won our fair share of possession during the match, but not in the right areas of the field, and we managed to disrupt the quality of their ball from the scrum. There were also some outstanding individual performances, but the fact that we had managed to push them all the way with so little preparation time and the way we fought back collectively was most encouraging for us coaches.

As was our custom we met as coaches on the Sunday following the Australia game to analyse aspects of individual and team performances, and also to ask groups of players to specifically look at particular aspects of the game. For example one of the props and a flanker might provide analysis of our defence of scrums, the hooker and one of the second rows could have the task of examining our lineout performance etc. Players too were expected to look through their own individual performances on the lap-tops and compile relevant statistics, in readiness for a complete team de-brief with the coaching staff on the Monday.

We made quite a few changes to the team for the game against the South Sea Islanders the following week, knowing that the last match, against New Zealand, was always going to be the most important game of that autumn series. It was therefore obviously in our interest to change the team and our tactics following the Wallabies match. This would give us an opportunity to look at different players and various combinations, and also ensure that the All Blacks would not be able to familiarise themselves too much with our patterns of play in the run-up to our encounter with them. We decided that our tactics would be to keep it a bit tighter against the Islanders and frustrate them, leading them to lose discipline and consequently to infringe.

The South Sea Islanders formed a combined team of players who weren't used to playing together and that was particularly evident during the first half. We succeeded in dominating possession at the set pieces, winning, at one stage, five lineouts in succession on our opponents' ball. Competing against opposition ball in the lineout has never traditionally been one of our strong points and maybe we don't earmark sufficient time in practice to address this particular aspect of play. Indeed the need to focus on winning your own ball is so great that giving attention to winning opposition ball is perhaps deemed to be of secondary importance. It had been recognised that, looking ahead to future games, we needed to find a balance in our approach to the lineouts as it is such a competitive area in the modern game and our success in this particular aspect of the area that afternoon was hugely encouraging.

At half time we led comfortably by 31–5 but saw the visitors rally well in the second half, during which they scored 15 points to our 7. It was a little disappointing that we didn't produce a more convincing performance after the break. But, as often happens with a side that has been outplayed in the opening period, they came out for the second half with a 'nothing to lose' attitude. There is also sometimes a tendency for teams well ahead at a particular stage of the game to relax a little and take their foot off the pedal. In any event, the final score was 38–20 and, bearing in mind the changes that had been made, it was a satisfying win.

With regard to our preparations for the game against Canada on November 17th we concentrated on the positive aspects of our play in the previous week's game against the South Sea Islanders and again followed the same analysis exercise on the visitors' performance in their recent matches. We had a fairly good idea of the way they played the game since we'd had quite a few matches against Canada in recent years and some of their players were now playing in Europe. Even though they weren't at their strongest due to players having club commitments, we realised the importance of getting a win and putting in a good performance. We dominated territory and possession during the match, and were again successful as a pack in disrupting the opposition lineout. We scored 9 tries in our total of 61 points but one area of concern was that we gave away a number of penalties and conceded 26 points in all, despite the fact that we'd had a presentation on the match official from one of our own referees, so that we could have some indication of the way he was likely to interpret the rules. However, this is not a foolproof means of ensuring that we know in advance how the referee is going to react in various situations, since there will always be grey areas with regard to law interpretation. For example, if a referee shouts "Hands away!" at the breakdown, is he directing this warning at the tackled player on the ground or is it directed at the opposing player standing over him? In any event the win against Canada was good for the morale of the team yet at the same time we knew that there wasn't much we could take from that game with regard to our forthcoming pool match against them in the 2007 World Cup.

Our remaining fixture that autumn, against the All Blacks, was always going to be the most difficult one. We knew, having watched footage of recent performances by the All Blacks, that they would bring an intensity that we hadn't yet encountered in our recent matches. The tackle area would therefore need to be focused on, and we obviously had to make slight adjustments and improvements on our set pieces to ensure that we could provide enough quality possession for our backs to play with.

The number of sessions where there was a forwards / backs split during that week were limited but when it did happen each coach would be expected to stick to his allotted time so that the players would not be overworked. Working on our fitness and conditioning was not a priority at this particular stage and maintaining a balance in our preparation was crucial so that the players were energised going in to the game. We would meet regularly as coaches and discuss the content of the sessions so as to make them as efficient as possible, and Mark Bennett, our conditioning coach, would be responsible for the timings during those sessions.

The drama that is usually associated with games between Wales and New Zealand was increased on this occasion by the controversy surrounding the *hakka*. The visitors had been requested to perform their traditional challenge prior to the singing of the Welsh National Anthem, which they were unwilling to do. They wanted to proceed directly to the game from the psychological 'high' they obviously derived from performing the *hakka*, with the adrenalin still in full flow. The Wales management team wanted to derive a similar advantage from the emotion stirred by our own national anthem, 'Mae Hen Wlad Fy Nhadau'. As a result the All Blacks decided to perform the *hakka* in their changing room beneath the stadium and the WRU were accused of scuppering one of the most popular rugby traditions in the world and of denying the huge crowd the pleasure of the customary dramatic performance. I think it would be fair to say that the attitude of the Wales management team was that if there is any psychological advantage to be gained from pre-kick-off procedures then any visiting team must expect to bend to the wishes of the home union. In that respect it would have been interesting, had we won that particular game, to see how other nations would subsequently have reacted to such a situation. As it happened the whole episode turned out to be an 'own goal' against us, since the big screens in the stadium, over which the management team has no control, transmitted the All Blacks performing their *hakka* in isolation before taking the field. They were consequently able to derive a moral victory from the incident which served also to win for them the sympathy of many in the crowd.

In light of the intensity with which the visitors approached the game from the outset, however, they obviously needed no sympathy at all! Despite winning plenty of possession, from our lineout in particular where our success rate was 95 per cent, and the scrum, we were under a lot of pressure. Where we found ourselves second best by a country mile was at the contact area. We had worked hard in training on this aspect since the Australia match but were still finding it hard to stop opposition players having an effect on our contact efficiencies. There is no doubt that we were given important lessons to learn during the All Blacks match. Firstly, they attacked us in the scrum in a particular way that meant we were under intense pressure throughout in that particular aspect. Seeing what had been one of our major building blocks in previous games crumble came as a bit of a shock. Secondly, even though our total time in possession of the ball was seven minutes longer than that of the All Blacks, we were turned over at the breakdown on 12 occasions, showing that unless effective use can be made of the possession obtained, there is not much point in having it!

We were losing by 3–23 at half time and, despite the fact that our pack came more into the game during the second period, the final score of 10–45 obviously reflected that we had been outplayed on the day. There were, however, some positive aspects that we could derive from the encounter. For example, the performance of James Hook, who took the field when Stephen Jones was injured, was very encouraging once again. There was also the fact that, during the latter part of the game, we managed to drive the All Blacks back over their own line from a lineout for our only try. Crumbs of comfort maybe, but this was both a blow to All Blacks' pride and to some extent a reflection of our durability in the face of adversity.

Following the series of matches we, as a coaching team, were keen to give feedback to the regions on the outcome of our endeavours during the previous weeks. On this occasion we had to delay that procedure for a week however, as immediately after the New Zealand game, all members of our coaching team were given a week's course on management skills and reaction to pressure as part of our development. We were introduced to systems, procedures and processes that would enable us to function more effectively as a group. The course was extremely useful and a member of the Ashridge team, a sports psychologist by the name of John Neal, was subsequently invited to join our management group. Gareth Jenkins could see that this appointment would help him fill a void which he felt had existed in the make-up of our team up until that time.

CHAPTER 15

# A Trying Time

Lots of people want to ride with you in the limo, but what you
want is someone who will take the bus with you when the limo
breaks down.

**Oprah Winfrey**

WE MET WITH each of the regional coaches following our
course in order to share our experiences and discuss
with them the lessons we had learnt so that they were aware
of the areas that we felt needed addressing. There was no
doubt that the need for good contact efficiencies at the tackle
area was one the most important messages, as it held the key
to the open rugby we wanted to play. I was also keen to stress
the importance of the scrum following the New Zealand
match in particular since I was aware of the amount of detail
that went in to the coaches' preparation.

When I was in the company of Mike Cron during my time
with the All Blacks in Ireland he showed me some of the benefits
that his academy props were able to derive from such disciplines
as gymnastics and judo. He was of the opinion that many of
the demands and skills of these sports could be of assistance
to rugby players, especially front row forwards. In his opinion
their most important contribution was to nurture functional
strength as opposed to developing strength measured against,
for example, a weighted bar or a pulley. This was not so much a
new way of thinking but rather a realisation of what was perhaps
overlooked initially with the introduction of so much weight
training to the modern rugby players' conditioning programme.
One of the aims would be to teach players how to make full use

of their strength when 'wrestling' or 'manhandling' an opponent, as you do in the game of rugby. I remember one of my lasting impressions when I first got involved in the national squad was seeing Brian Williams, Kevin Phillips and John Davies all sitting at a table following a day of fitness testing, tucking in to their food with their biceps bulging. They may not have been the strongest at pushing or pulling a bar in a straight line but I can't think of better examples of players with the ability to rip the ball from a maul. As a result of long hours spent working on the farm, all three, no doubt, could transfer that functional strength on to the field, something which must also have helped John win the 'Wales' Strongest Man' title in 1993, a year after my success, although he somehow got away with receiving less 'stick' than I'd had.

In order to explore this avenue further, I got in touch with Neil Adams MBE, who had won numerous Olympic and Judo World Championship medals, and who currently works with the Wales National Judo Team. Following a couple of meetings with him, during which I illustrated how I thought some rugby situations might benefit from judo techniques, he agreed to help us out. Some of the players weren't convinced at first but, having extracted instances that illustrated the similarity between actual match confrontations and judo moves, we convinced the doubters that there was a definite link between certain aspects of both disciplines. Neil did quite a bit of work with us at the time and we immediately began to see the benefits during training, and in due course, during our matches.

It was important for us to kick off the Six Nations with a win against Ireland, especially as our next three matches were all away. It was definitely a game we could have won as we had more possession than Ireland and were in their 22 on no fewer than 18 occasions. There was dissatisfaction in some quarters that Kevin Deaker, the referee, hadn't sufficiently penalised

Ireland for slowing down our possession from rucks and mauls, but you don't win games by complaining about the referee. We often let frustration get the better of us, with the result that our use of the possession we had was disappointing. There was, however, 'one of those moments', when Wales were trailing by only 12–9, which could have turned the game following a period of intense Welsh pressure. A penalty could well have been given against Ireland for bringing down Chris Czekaj as the winger endeavoured to gather the ball with the Irish line at his mercy, but the visitors survived and surged upfield to add to their own score with another try, thus securing a 17–9 victory. This meant that we were up against it in the championship from the word 'go', and that we were going to have to regroup quickly for the following week.

Next up was our match against Scotland and time was against us in our preparations as we had a short turnaround; having played Ireland on the Sunday, we were due to play in Scotland on the Saturday. The players had two days to recover after the Ireland game from their bumps and bruises and to enable those that suffered injuries to receive physiotherapy treatment. As a result we were able to do very little as a team on those two days, which left us one full day's training before travelling up to Edinburgh. With regard to selection we had little choice in certain positions and so we decided to make changes to give us enough energy on the field. The boys coming into the team would need some time to settle in, and we were confident that they would be up to speed by the Saturday. In our debrief at the end of the Six Nations, however, we reflected that it would have been of greater benefit had we delayed our departure for Scotland until that evening to give us an extra training session in the morning and therefore more time to prepare. The upshot of such a hectic week was that we had little time to change the game plan we had adopted against Ireland and Scotland knew that full well!

The first scrum at Murrayfield epitomised the pattern of the whole game. The way we were pushed off the ball so destructively was indeed an eyebrow raiser and I am still unable to analyse what happened; not even the players involved could tell me. It was a huge psychological boost for Scotland and a massive blow for us. From that point on, the home team went from strength to strength and completely dominated possession. They had done their homework on us in the lineout and, in Scott Murray, they possessed one of the best defensive lineout jumpers in the world with the result that he continually and effectively disrupted our ball in that area. In our frustration at not being able to get our hands on the ball, we conceded twice as many penalties as our opponents (17 in total), for which Chris Patterson made us pay, giving Scotland a 21–9 victory. The one small consolation for us that afternoon was that our defensive commitment was such that they failed to cross our line.

Of course we should have done better on the day. On occasions, wrong options were called on the field with regard to certain moves we had in our armoury. Nevertheless, when players make decisions on the field of play, as coaches we have to stand by those decisions. I firmly believe that, as a player, you develop a feel for the game and you are therefore often in a better position than the coach to assess the situation. Whatever decision the player makes at the time, be it right or wrong, I would support that decision and then discuss it with him so that he's aware of what to do should he find himself in a similar situation in future.

After the first five minutes that afternoon, there was a huge question being asked of our forwards as to how they were going to react for the remainder of the game. There was no doubt that our confidence had been rocked and we could well have folded completely but, to the players' credit, we continued to compete, albeit without success, to keep us within striking distance of our opponents right until the end. In our debrief as forwards we highlighted the errors in our game as well as focusing on the positives. We reminded ourselves of where we were as recently as the previous autumn and that we weren't a million miles off the required standard of play. The personnel had more or less remained the same and we believed that it was only a matter of time before the efforts of all concerned would be rewarded. Naturally, the morale of the squad was a little low following the defeat and especially in view of the manner in which we lost, but it was now a case of preparing for the match two weeks later in Paris, against one of the leading sides in world rugby. We knew that we would be up against a very strong pack in Paris, and that we needed to focus on improving our set piece that had been so disappointing against Scotland.

There was a long day of hanging around in the hotel on match day, prior to facing France, due to a nine o'clock kick off. This allowed me time to meet with each of the forwards in the squad for a five-minute chat to discuss how they thought the preparations during the previous two weeks had gone, and to clear up any queries that they might have had on their particular role that day. More importantly it was an opportunity to give each individual the confidence to go out and 'do the business' against the French. Ironically we were only awarded six scrums during the whole game in France but we were able to provide a solid platform from those, along with the lineout, where it was so important for us to regain our confidence and composure. We started the match well, scoring two tries in the first quarter, but then allowed France back in to the game before half time, going in to the break with the scores at 23–14. As forwards we had identified that one of the strengths of the French forward play was the rolling maul, especially from their lineouts. We knew that we could ill afford allowing them to gain momentum by using this tactic and decided to make sure we stopped this threat at source. I'm aware that supporters often get frustrated when they see their team not competing for the ball on the opposition's throw, but it can be an effective way of stopping the opposition if its done properly. We succeeded in doing this, along with turning them over eight times at the breakdown. This was not enough however, as France dominated territory and possession during the match, winning 32–21 at the final whistle, even though we outscored them on tries.

We obviously looked to build and improve on the performance in Paris, having gained some of our confidence back. As with France we expected Italy to be very strong at forward and once again we were aware that they employed the driving maul to get the crowd behind them. With that in mind, we attempted to keep the ball in open play as much as possible in order to deny Italy the opportunity of employing rolling mauls from the lineouts that would ensue from our kicking to touch. On reflection we perhaps should have balanced this with kicking for territorial advantage more often, since our opponents had dominated that area. Possession also went against us, with Italy winning twice as many rucks and mauls as Wales.

Much was made of referee Chris White's 'blunder' at the close, when, by blowing the final whistle, he prevented us from taking a lineout five metres from the Italian try line, having indicated initially that more time remained. But we should never have been in that situation. The crucial factor for us coaches was that we had won enough possession and territory in the last ten minutes to have enabled us to win, but we conceded the ball too often, failing to hold on to it in order to go through the phases. Also, in the closing stages, we were penalised on more than one occasion, unfairly so in my opinion, thereby forcing us to surrender attacking positions from which we should have won the game. The loss was again hugely disappointing for all of us, even though we knew that things were improving. Our players had shown a lot of character during recent matches and were still growing as individuals and as a team in the international arena.

We had one match left and even though the England game was, in a manner of speaking, our last chance saloon there were one or two factors to spur us on. Firstly, having been on the road for three consecutive games we were at home at last, which is always a significant advantage and, of course, seeking to beat England, 'the old enemy', was in itself a powerful focus. Perhaps that shouldn't be the case but it is simply a fact that cannot be ignored. History has conditioned us to believe that victory against England will always be sweeter and our supporters, along with our national press, contribute to that psyche. The downside of this standpoint, of course, is that more pressure rests on the players and the coaching staff to get it right for that particular match.

And get it right we did, on a day when everything clicked, to enable us to gain a notable 27–18 win! Our set piece was particularly strong thus giving us good possession to attack from, and disrupted theirs in the process. In broken play we competed well at the breakdown, turning them over six times, and made over twice as many offloads as England in attack. As a result, we were able to play our style of rugby, relished by players such as James Hook, and in doing so he became only the second Welsh player, after Neil Jenkins in Paris in 2001, to score in every possible way in one match. The sense of relief for all concerned at the end of the match was so obvious and the emotions so high! It was good to know that what we'd been trying to achieve for months had materialised at last and so pleasing to receive confirmation that we were indeed on the right path for greater success. The only frustration was that we weren't due to face anyone the following week, to see whether we could have maintained the momentum.

Players don't usually sleep well following matches, particularly important ones. The adrenalin in their bodies is in full flow for hours afterwards, in addition to which the caffeine tablets, which they are encouraged to take some hours before kick off to sharpen their senses and heighten their awareness, take a long time to lose their potency. My reasons for being awake during the night of the England game were different. As I had done with regard to the other Six Nations fixtures earlier in the season I got up during the early hours to join our analysts who were working through the night to produce a coded version of the previous afternoon's match. From this version I picked out examples that would help me to analyse what exactly had happened in certain contexts within the game. This material was then available for presentation and discussion at the debrief meeting to be held with the players that morning before they departed for home, at the end of a testing six-week campaign.

Despite the poor results it was a campaign that left me in a positive mood. I thought that, apart from the Scotland game, which was the kind of inexplicable nightmare that happens to all sportsmen at some stage, we put ourselves in a strong position to win the matches. Bearing in mind also that we, as coaches, viewed the Six Nations in this particular instance as an opportunity to see, and work with, a number of young players in readiness for the World Cup Competition, we could take heart from what was achieved during the early part of 2007. From a personal perspective one of the important lessons that I learned from my first Six Nations Championship as a coach was that you have to remain true to yourself, particularly when the going gets tough. You must stand by what you believe to be right, have confidence in the people around you and hope that the strength of your own convictions will rub off on them.

# CHAPTER 16

# Dark Days

*Every body has a need for heroes, I think, people to mould themselves after, people they want to be like. You have to be able to dream, but those dreams should be about real people who have actually done things.*

**Dave Thomas**

TOWARDS THE END of the 2006-7 season, the news concerning Ray Gravell, that it had been necessary, firstly to amputate his toes, and later the lower part of his left leg, came as a huge shock. I had been aware for some time that Gravs had been suffering from the ill effects of diabetes, such as weight loss, during the Six Nations. We saw each other regularly during the pre- and post-match interviews on S4C, and would always share a joke and have a laugh. Regardless of the circumstances, Gravs always seemed to have that knack of leaving you with a smile on your face – even mine! That was true even when I rang him at the hospital in Carmarthen soon after the initial surgery, mindful of the fact that he was probably being inundated with calls and visitors. I was anticipating a chat with Mari, his wife, so that I could spare Gravs, in his weakened condition, the strain of having to answer the same questions for the umpteenth time. Within seconds of getting through Gravs himself had insisted on taking the call and, although my intention had been to enquire about his condition, most of the conversation was taken up with my having to answer Grav's questions as to the wellbeing of my family, how my sons were doing etc. It was so typical of him, in the midst of his personal suffering, to be more concerned about others.

When I was first accepted to the National Eisteddfod Gorsedd of Bards in 2006 I had been teased by Gravs, who was the official sword-bearer of the Gorsedd, that I should, perhaps, consider taking over his particular duty in the future. Gravs had initially agreed to perform that task for a period of ten years and, since the 2006 Eisteddfod was the ninth occasion for him to do so, he was now looking for a replacement! Little did we know at the time that the unfortunate circumstances of his illness would mean that I would need to stand in for him during the 2007 Eisteddfod ceremonies. I had been officially approached by a family friend, the Rev. John Gwilym Jones, the Gorsedd Recorder and a former Archdruid, as to whether I would be prepared to accept that duty at the Proclamation Ceremony of the 2008 Cardiff National Eisteddfod, to be held on 16th June, 2007, and at the National Eisteddfod in Flintshire the following August.

When it was confirmed that I was to stand in for Gravs, I was naturally keen to consult him to find out what exactly was required of me. I then went to see him at his home in Mynydd y Garreg, where three crews from various branches of the media, all doing programmes on Gravs, wished to record the occasion. My arrival was greeted with Gravs, who'd been running around after his daughters upstairs, bouncing down the stairs and expressing his delight that I had been given the honour in question. During my visit, and during the interviews, he made sure that I appreciated its importance and to that end he even gave me a brief history lesson. He told me that the first Eisteddfod ever was held in 1176 in Cardigan, organised by Lord Rhys whose mother, the princess Gwenllian, was killed leading an army of Welshmen against the Normans at Cydweli Castle, a stone's throw from Gravs's home. The incident, commemorated by the subsequent naming of the site where that particular battle took place as Gwenllian Court was, to Gravs, a source of great local and national pride.

Until recently, even though I had competed at the National Eisteddfod, I was never a keen follower nor particularly appreciative of its cultural and historical significance for the Welsh people. When I was invited to become a member of the Gorsedd, my father impressed upon me that it was a great honour and one of the highest my own country could bestow on me. I had some reservations about my duties initially, most of which stemmed from my ignorance of Gorsedd protocol and my lack of knowledge of 'who's who' in the eisteddfodic hierarchy. However, I received a lot of help from various Gorsedd members, and also benefited from the knowledge I acquired by listening to the comprehensive coverage by Radio Cymru of matters concerning the Eisteddfod. Above all, the encouragement given me by Gravs was invaluable and I was so pleased to see him in the audience during my first sword-bearing ceremony on the Monday, for the official opening of the Eisteddfod. I thoroughly enjoyed my duties at Mold where I increasingly appreciated both the importance of the National Eisteddfod's role in upholding the values, traditions and culture of Welsh-speaking Wales and also the extent of the honour that had come my way. Having lived and worked in many different areas of the country, I'm prepared to accept that the National Eisteddfod doesn't necessarily mean as much to everyone in Wales, but to me it represents the Wales that I know and with which I identify.

The early part of the summer had been taken up with preparing for the Wales tour to Australia, where we were to play two Tests. The selection of the squad was the subject of much debate but the bottom line was that there were a number of senior experienced players who were both physically and mentally tired after a long season and would benefit from a break before preparations for the World Cup began in earnest. In addition we were keen to learn more about many younger players and to assess them as to how they would react to the pressures of performing on an international stage. In any event we believed that we would be able to select from that squad a team that was good enough not just to compete, but also to beat Australia.

The Australian press gave us a hard time from the moment we arrived. Firstly they accused us of undermining the value of the tour, especially for Australian rugby followers, by selecting our 'second' team. In particular they continually complained about our apparent 'inaccessibility', in that we had chosen to make our base at a hotel on the sea shore in the Terrigal area, which is around an hour and a half's drive away from Sydney. In fact Alan Phillips, our team Manager, had chosen the location during a preliminary visit some months earlier, precisely because it was comparatively distant and remote thereby enabling us to concentrate almost exclusively on our match preparations without any distraction. We had expected such 'attacks' and took this ranting by the press with a pinch of salt for we were fully aware of the country's tendency to resort to mind-games prior to major sporting encounters. After all, we'd had Scott Johnson in our camp for some time!

We couldn't have wished for a better start in the First Test – we were 17-0 ahead after 20 minutes before Australia began to claw their way back. The major stumbling block for us was the scrum and in particular the way South African referee Jonathan Kaplan interpreted the engagement rule. It was obvious that Australia were anticipating the call to engage and were gaining an advantage by beating us to the hit. In the Northern hemisphere, we were used to referees varying the speed and tempo of their commands to prevent this very problem from happening and it was clearly dangerous since the Wales pack weren't ready for the hit. As a result we were unable to settle or impose ourselves at all at the scrum. Yet we were in the lead almost until the final whistle and losing that First Test, by 23–29, was a big disappointment as we were within a whisker of beating Australia on their own patch for the first time ever. The opportunity was lost purely as a result of our lack of composure in the dying stages of the game.

If nothing else we had, however, proved to ourselves and others that we were good enough and that there was perhaps a greater depth in strength with regards to selection that many had at first thought.

It was again a case of having to manage training during the week so that we could work on areas that we felt had been exposed and also keeping the players fresh for the Second Test. We had injuries and new personnel to contend with, which resulted in having to play Ceri Jones at tight-head, where his experience was limited. Mefin Davies had also flown out to replace Mathew Rees (who had returned home for personal reasons), and hadn't had much time to prepare with the rest of the pack, so we had to work smart.

We had exactly the same problem with the scrum in the Second Test, even though we'd met with referee Paul Honiss and discussed with him the fact that Australia had constantly anticipated the call to engage in that First Test. We were outplayed for most of the game, trailing by just 6–0 at half time before losing eventually by 31–0. It had been evident that there were many Welsh players on the field that day who, after a very hard encounter in the First Test and an even harder domestic season, felt jaded and stale. So, in some respects, the tour was one step too far for many of the players. For the coaches, however, it proved to be an excellent opportunity to get to know players better and assess who was able to withstand the pressures of such a tour and who amongst them would be contenders for World Cup selection.

Yet I have to confess that towards the end of that final week, rugby, for me, became of secondary importance. Following a routine phone call to my parents on the Tuesday, I learnt that my father had been taken ill. Both he and my mother regularly attended a fitness centre at Bangor and while there, he had complained of chest pains. My mother took him to the local hospital where he underwent some tests and despite him carrying his own kit bag from the gym to the car, and eating a hearty lunch at the hospital, the tests showed that he would have to be transferred to a special unit at Broadgreen Hospital as soon as possible. He insisted that my mother was not to accompany him in the ambulance nor to follow in her own car but that he would telephone her that evening. When he did so it was to say that he would be going to theatre for an operation the following morning and that he would see my mother later that day.

He had also made my mother promise that on no condition was I to be told of the extent of his illness nor was my tour schedule to be disrupted in any way. So during my telephone calls to her she tried very hard to conceal the seriousness of the illness by saying that it was a case now of waiting for the results of a number of tests that had been done but that otherwise things were fine. When I spoke to my sister and to Tina concerning my father's condition, they too did their best to play it down. However, I had begun to suspect that the situation was serious so I sought the advice of Professor John Williams, the tour Medical Officer. He kindly got in touch with some contacts he had in the medical world and was eventually able to speak by telephone with the relevant staff at Broadgreen Hospital immediately after the Second Test (the time difference between the two countries meant that it wasn't possible to get through to the appropriate department before then). John told me that my father, having suffered a pulmonary aneurysm, had undergone a huge operation a few days previously and that he still hadn't come round. I rang both my mother and Tina and was then made fully aware of what had happened.

The flight home on the Sunday, with its three transfers en route, seemed to exacerbate my desperation to get home as quickly as possible, to hopefully see my father and be with the family. During the journey I made several calls in order to keep abreast of my father's condition and the family did their best to put up an optimistic front, with mention of an 'apparent' response from time to time. I arrived in Tumble late Monday afternoon, where Tina confirmed that the situation was very grave and, after spending some time with our children, we both travelled to my parents' house at Brynrefail. From there my sister Beth and I drove immediately to the hospital in Broadgreen where we spent the night at my father's bedside, holding his hand. I was still trying to be positive and did my best not to contemplate the finality of the hospital's prognosis, which was even more difficult to accept upon seeing my father lying there, an apparent picture of health. The family had been trying desperately to get him to respond, by singing, reading, talking etc. but to no avail. Tests had been performed the previous Saturday to determine whether there was any hope of my father surviving. The results were negative, but it was apparently common practice to run a final set of tests twenty-four hours later. If they, too, were negative it meant that there was no hope of survival and every means of artificial life-support would be withdrawn. The family had requested that final test to be delayed until after my arrival at the hospital.

The result was, unfortunately, a foregone conclusion and the painful decision to authorise the hospital to switch off the respirator had to be made, leaving in its wake a tremendous sense of loss. I'd always relied heavily on my father, not only for advice and guidance but also for his active support throughout my career. For a short time after his death, I felt a great loss of purpose and direction, which was natural as I still drew upon him for advice even as a coach. More importantly, perhaps, I was also able to seek his guidance on all aspects of life and his influence in that respect will, of course, remain. As a person he was very private and unassuming and got on quietly with whatever had to be done. He always went out of his way to help others and made a point of never criticising anyone in public. As a coach I have tried to adopt some of these attributes in my dealings with the players under my supervision. Indeed they are features which are often prominent in successful pupil/teacher relationships and it was a source of great satisfaction to us as a family that so many of my father's former pupils were at his funeral. There were many others who, although unable to be present, wrote kindly of his influence on their childhood, including one who was a pupil at Llangefni School, in the very first class that my father taught upon leaving Bangor Normal College.

At the funeral, Naomi, Beth and myself read poems that we felt expressed the feelings we had for our father, how proud we were of him and how much of an influence he'd had on us all. My mother stood for well over an hour following the service, greeting and thanking everybody for their presence and condolences. I'd like to think that my father would have been proud of us all on the day, and I received the best compliment possible hearing so many people comment on how alike we both were.

In keeping with my father's custom of helping others, if at all possible, he had been a blood donor for many years and carried an organ donor card. As a result, we have been given to understand, as a family, that there have been four recipients of some of my father's organs hitherto, one of whom was in danger of losing his life unless a suitable kidney donor could be found. In fact, a short time ago he wrote to my mother expressing his deep gratitude and described how the transplant had both saved and changed his life. As a family we have drawn comfort from the fact that others have been able to benefit from our great loss and also from the fact that my father's wish to become a donor was completely in keeping with the way he lived his life.

# CHAPTER 17

# The Build Up and the Fall

If no-one ever took risks, Michelangelo would have painted
the Sistine floor.

**Neil Simon**

THE PERIOD FOLLOWING our return from Australia was initially taken up with discussions concerning the possible make-up of our World Cup squad and our planning requirements regarding the tournament itself. The players had been split into four groups to ensure that they all received the same attention, and to maximize the benefits of all the conditioning work they were doing. I also began working with the forwards, including those who hadn't toured with us to Australia, on the basic skills that would be required at the set piece. In the scrum we concentrated on body positions and technique, focusing in particular on lowering our height pre- and post-engagement. At the lineout we worked on speeding up all the components – jumping, lifting and throwing, regardless of the particular systems that would be used during the games to come.

At the end of July the whole squad moved to Brittany where we spent a week at the Ker Juliette Hotel in Pornichet, which was also to be our base when playing our Pool matches in Nantes in September. It had a magnificent sea-front location near La Baule and excellent facilities incorporating suitable amenities for our needs. We had separate rooms for the physio, masseur, analysts, a meeting room for the coaches, and a team room for the players with a projector to view any films that had been arranged by the entertainments committee. The team room also had internet access, which allowed the players to fill in their daily online diaries and keep in touch with their families and friends via e-mail. The hotel also had a swimming pool and a tennis court, but what proved to be most popular was cycling, since the hotel provided an ample supply of bikes for our use. Indeed the road to La Baule, a twenty minute ride away, must have been an awesome sight some evenings as our pack of Tour de France wannabees headed for the town's *crêperies* to sample their *crêpes*!

Diet requirements and training facilities were two other all-important matters to be considered. Bringing our own chef with us, Bernie, who had been responsible for our meals in the past, ensured the former. The latter was provided by the local rugby club at St. Nazaire, a third division club in the French Championship. The club's practice amenities, particularly the quality of its pitches, were excellent and surpassed the standard that any of our four regional clubs can offer in Wales.

The emphasis on our preparations as a squad had now begun to turn to the playing aspect and we began to step up the intensity by engaging in full contact drills during training. As the set-piece coach, I considered that there were a number of things that needed to be ironed out, both with regard to the scrum and the lineout. We had to make sure that each member of the pack was comfortable with his particular role with regard to the tactics being employed in the scrum. In the lineout, we'd used a number of different systems during the past year, so we could analyse our performance in that area and conclude what had and hadn't been successful. As a result we were able to identify that our most effective lineouts were the ones that had the least amount of movement, so we focused on these options in our training. We also worked on our defensive options and reactions on opposition ball, both when staying down and competing on our opponents' throw. Clarity was needed regarding our calling system to ensure efficiency, which meant our lineout attack and defence captains (usually our second rows), had to work out the right options. Similarly, our tighthead and loosehead props would serve as scrum attack and scrum defence captains.

By the time we had completed our week's stay in Brittany, we as coaches had a fairly good idea of who would form the hard core of the pack in our 30-man World Cup squad. But before that squad was chosen, we were due to play England at Twickenham, giving us a final opportunity to look at some of the players we were still unsure about. Much criticism ensued over the team that represented Wales that day, which wasn't our strongest team of course, and the resultant scoreline was a blow to morale in the run-up to the World Cup, as we were hammered 62–7. There were arguments for and against such a selection and, had we suffered an injury to any of our key players at such a late stage, I'm sure we would have also been criticised for playing them. I would still maintain that we did the right thing by going for the players in question to face England as there were still a number of them we were unsure of as to whether they would be able to deliver on the international stage. Unfortunately, in that respect, the performance on the day left a lot to be desired and, ironically, ultimately made the selection of the final squad much easier. It also questioned the strength in depth that we thought we possessed following the First Test in Australia earlier that summer. As expected, following such a disappointing result, there were many negatives to the game from our point of view as coaches. We had spent so much time defending that we hadn't been able to assess how good we were in attack, the forwards being unable to win any quality ball. The fact that the defeat was against England, of all teams, made it that much harder to stomach. I would stress, however, that no other members of the squad, at that stage, would have been better prepared than those who played at Twickenham. But it must be accepted that our discipline was sadly lacking, having given away a number of penalties which allowed England some eight or nine opportunities to drive 5-metre lineouts during the game. The only positive for us was that they managed to score from only two of those, which at least highlighted our capacity to defend in adversity.

During the two weeks between that game and our forthcoming encounter with Argentina the final squad of thirty players had been named for the World Cup, which meant that we were now able to work fully with two packs and consequently able to pay more attention to detail as to how our lineout and scrum systems were working. The match against England had highlighted the areas that we needed to work on and we sought to use that experience as a learning opportunity in advance of the World Cup competition. In particular we needed to become more 'streetwise' at the lineout and needed to improve our composure and all round game management when under pressure.

The Argentina game served as a timely test to see, in particular, whether we had benefited from our mistakes in the previous game. I was particularly pleased with the performance of the forwards in the first half, against a pack that contained seven of the eight forwards that started the World Cup semi-final for Argentina against South Africa two months later. Our defensive lineout worked well and we brought composure and rhythm to the lineout in attacking situations. The scrum, too, was a source of quality possession for us, which meant that all the work we had done in the those areas where we'd been exposed by England two weeks previously had paid off, and that we had learnt our lesson. Having dominated most of the possession we went in at half-time with a comfortable 24–3 lead. However the visitors saw much more of the ball during the second half and we were drawn into a kicking game which we didn't manage at all well. Despite tremendous pressure on our line during the last few minutes we were very relieved to win by 27–20, but it had been a gutsy performance by Wales.

One of our main considerations, in preparing for the game against France a week later, and looking ahead to our opening game of the World Cup, was consistency in selection. We'd looked in detail at the French performance in their games against England a few weeks previously and made a note of certain features of their play. Of the three teams we encountered in August, France certainly made the biggest impression on us. From the forwards point of view, we familiarised ourselves with the type of lineouts which they favoured most and who their main jumpers were, as their back five were all pretty athletic and good jumpers to boot. They all possessed an abundance of skill and flair and were as powerful as the Argentinians but without their rough edges.

Whereas we were quite happy with the way we handled our set pieces and with the amount of possession we gained as a result, the French defence was magnificent. We had difficulty, time after time, in crossing the gain line and lost the battle in the contact area, where we were prone to commit too many of our players to the breakdown, leading to France often having superior numbers on the counter attack. In addition our kicking game wasn't up to scratch, which frequently gave our opponents the opportunity to run back at us, which they did effectively and clinically. It was a resounding victory for them, by 34–7. Yet we weren't too dismayed, even in the light of that defeat, since in many areas of our game the relevant statistics showed that we were continuing to progress and also that France, in our opinion, were going to be one of the strongest teams in the forthcoming competition.

We returned to Brittany, therefore, in a fairly buoyant mood and received a fantastic welcome. Local schoolchildren greeted us at the airport with red berets for each member of our party, the hotel staff at Pornichet were obviously very pleased to have us as guests once again and at the St. Nazaire Rugby Club a crowd of some 1,000 local people came to watch our practice session. We were fortunate that we had survived without any major injury problems and it was good to see a buzz about the players, such as Stephen Jones, who was taking a full part in training for the first time since his injury. Our selection process was the same as usual. We as coaches would all sit down to discuss each of the players in contention for places, with each of us giving our views on those players' qualities and, possibly, deficiencies with regard to the particular aspects of play for which we as individual coaches were responsible. In my case, therefore, my primary concern was the way in which the forwards in question performed in the set pieces but, at selection meetings, those forwards' merits were also analysed in the light of the attacking and defensive requirements noted by Nigel and Rowland. Gareth would then listen to these views and contribute to our discussions. He would then go away to ponder and ultimately to select the team, before discussing his final choice with us.

For our first game against Canada our aim was to constrain our opponents at first phase. We believed we could dominate the scrums, win our lineout ball comfortably and target their throw effectively. In addition, we were confident that our defensive system would nullify their attempts to attack. The game saw the birth of a recurring theme throughout our World Cup campaign for us, whereby our opening was quite promising only for our performance then to deteriorate for a lengthy period during the remainder of the first half. There was then an opportunity during the interval to regroup and re-visit the agreed game plan whereupon the third quarter would see the players produce a much better performance. Against Canada, in the first half, we failed to assert control as we should have. It had been decided that we didn't want to take them on up front, which would have meant playing to their strengths. But since we were unable to produce our own effective forward momentum our game became far too lateral as we tried to spread the ball wide with the result that at the interval we were trailing by 7–17. During the break I had a brief chat with our scrum and lineout captains in order to get their views on the set-piece performance so far, before all the players made their way in to see Gareth, Nigel and Rowland, who would address the team as a whole regarding the tactics going in to the second half.

Early on in the second half, it was decided to make some substitutions, which had an immediate effect. As is often the case, replacement players sitting in the stand are able to pinpoint any shortcomings more clearly than the players on the field and know what is required to rectify them. Consequently when Stephen Jones and Gareth Thomas came on they immediately put their experience and authority to good use and transformed the game. With the Canada team also tiring as a result of their constant need to defend we ultimately had a comfortable but all-important victory, by 42–17.

We knew, however, that we still had a lot of work to do before we could pose a threat to our next opponents, the Wallabies, at the Millennium Stadium one week later. We had, of course, encountered many of their players in the two Test matches we'd played in Australia a few months previously and knew they had very talented individuals whom we'd have to watch very carefully. They had a strong kicking game (which meant that our kicking game needed to be spot on), and brought tremendous physicality to the breakdown. In the set pieces, we'd worked hard to improve our engagement procedure in the scrums since conceding a number of penalties in that area when the two teams met in Australia and took confidence from our performance at the lineout in recent matches.

We made many errors during the first half, which meant

that we were trailing 25–3 at half-time. Once again, despite a reasonable supply of ball we were guilty of resorting too often to a lateral game, with the result that our ball carriers would frequently be stopped before crossing the gain line. If they attempted to offload, the next man would then, more often than not, receive both opposing player and ball. The knock on effect, since our opponents were so clinical at the breakdown, was that we would commit too many players to that area, which led to us trying to attack with smaller numbers than there were defending against us. Indeed in about 30 per cent of our rucks there were as many as seven of our players involved.

There were other aspects of our play that were disappointing, including our kicking game which was often found wanting. As far as our defence was concerned, we sought to employ a 'blitz' defence whereby we would run up quickly as a line to close down the Australian attack. This is a form of defence that hadn't always been adopted at our regional level, with the result that we didn't employ it as often as we would have liked.

There was a marked improvement in our performance during the second half, mainly because we fared much better in the contact area and made more effective use of our kicking game. Once again this seemed to follow the pattern we had established in all the Pool matches and statistics showed that, in our four games, we scored ten tries in all during the third quarter, compared to three by our opponents during that particular period of the game. By now we'd got used to 'chasing' games, which tended to make us play with a more relaxed attitude. We felt we were still in with a chance when we pulled the score back to 25–10 but luck was obviously against us when Stephen Jones failed to gather that Chris Latham kick, which bounced straight into the Australian's arms and allowed him to canter over the line. That, then, left us with too big a mountain to climb, and in the end, a feeling of great disappointment that we hadn't been able to put effectively into practice the pattern of play we had rehearsed in training.

Despite the disappointment of the Wallabies game we weren't going to dwell on it. Our outlook with regard to the next match, against Japan, was going to be different, mainly because the need to create a healthy competitive environment in the squad meant that different players now had to be given a chance. We also knew that Japan's approach to the game was unlike that which we'd experienced so far. Mainly as a result of their lack of bulk amongst their forwards, they preferred to play the game at a hundred miles an hour and away from the set pieces. We'd watched them against Fiji, a game they should have won, so we knew that we couldn't afford to take them lightly. We hoped to put pressure on them in those set pieces, particularly in the lineout, since height was a problem for them, where we would try to impose ourselves on their ball. The Japanese must have realised this, as during the match they countered our lineout by only putting three or four forwards in the line and they then used the rest of the pack to try and stop our peel into mid-field. We took this tactic as a compliment but it meant that we too had to change our tactics and opt for the catch-and-drive on our lineout ball.

We went into that game with a great deal of inner confidence and a feeling that it was going to be our day. And so it was, as a very commendable team performance gave us a satisfying 72–18 win, during which we scored eleven tries. Yet we had our usual initial scare as Japan twice took the lead during the opening period, the second time following one of the best tries of the World Cup by their winger Endo. That try came about after some poor decision making by us when, instead of walking the scrum comfortably over our opponents' line, we decided to pick the ball up at the base. The result was a turn-over, from which Japan scorched along the length of the field to score a magnificent try.

We were all glad, the morning after, to be leaving Cardiff for Brittany once again. There was such a favourable and comfortable World Cup 'ambience' in France and it had felt rather strange to have to turn our backs on it in mid-stream, as it were, to return to Wales, where we were placed once again under the microscope and subjected to disappointingly negative criticism from the press.

The day following our return to Pornichet the players took advantage of some down time and enjoyed a trip to Paris arranged by the Entertainments Committee and accompanied by two French liaison officers who had been assigned by the IRB to the Welsh party. The coaches stayed behind to work with the players who were recovering from injury and to start preparing for the Fiji game the following week. As coaches we had watched the Pool games in which Fiji had been engaged and noted that they were considerably more structured than they had been in the past. They were solid at the set piece and a number of talented individuals had excelled in their general play, including Nicky Little, the former Pontypriddd outside half, who was the shrewd operator of an effective kicking game. We sought to play a tight game, with the aim of frustrating them and causing them to concede a number of penalties, which would take us upfield and allow us to accumulate goal-kicking points when on offer. We also intended to kick to touch and pressurize their lineout and also to ensure that we didn't kick loosely from hand thereby enabling them to make ground by running back at us at their most dangerous.

Unfortunately, for whatever reason, so many of those tactics didn't happen on the field. The first ten minutes went according to plan but when we were then awarded penalties in their 22 we took quick tap-penalties. We didn't kick to touch, we didn't drive lineouts, nor did we make the most of our advantage in the scrum. Everything we had agreed, going into the game, that we were going to do, we failed to achieve on the pitch.

With the help of some stirring and athletic play in the loose, a lucky bounce or two and our inability to implement anything of note, Fiji shot to a 25–10 lead at half time. They had implemented a lot of the damage in the contact area, where we were unable to compete with their physicality. That particular weakness, along with our poor game management, were the main reasons why we did so badly against Fiji. Stephen Jones was desperately unlucky to see three of his place kicks hit the post that afternoon but the fact remained that our goal-kicking success rate over all the Pool games was only 64 per cent.

As usual during the interval we reiterated our game plan, pointing out where we were going wrong and, as usual, we had a great start to the second half. Decent possession, good handling and sharp running brought us right back into the game, so much so that we took the lead on two occasions, only for Fiji to seal the victory with a late try. During that last period the fact that we were unable to make the right decisions under pressure handed Fiji a deserved victory. One of the disappointing aspects of the Fiji fixture was comment frequently heard prior to the game, "After all Wales are *only* playing Fiji, so there should be no problem getting through to the last eight!" And then in the aftermath of that game there has been a tendency for people to discredit the Wales team purely and simply because they lost to Fiji.

But Fiji are a good side, ample proof of which is that they came within a whisker of beating the eventual champions, South Africa, in their next game. There were close games throughout the competition, with the so-called weaker teams raising their game and giving the favourites a run for their money. We shouldn't have had to rely on the bounce of the ball, nor the rebound off the post, to win but these 'moments' did have a bearing on the game.

There was a surreal atmosphere following the final whistle

as the realisation that we were out of the competition began to take effect. Just twenty-four hours previously we, as coaches, had started to make preparations for the game against South Africa in Marseilles a week later, since we would have been foolish not to plan ahead. Now we were on our way home and we, along with the players, were in a state of shock. There was a deathly hush in the changing room as the players sat in complete disbelief. Gareth Jenkins addressed the whole squad, pointing out that we couldn't have asked for any more effort but we had, without doubt, under-performed. He told us that, although not intending to resign, he had no idea as to what would happen regarding the future. Following the post-match function with the Fijians, who were naturally overjoyed as they entertained everybody with their customary singing, the squad, along with Gareth and us coaches, returned to the team room at the hotel. We spent a quiet, sombre night reliving the match and reflected on how different it could have been for us, and the lessons we had learned during the campaign. There was also the question of how we might best cope with the backlash that surely awaited us.

I had arranged to meet the forwards the following morning, prior to the team de-brief called for 10.45, so that I could give them my overall impression of their performance in the World Cup. I told them that with regard to the set pieces, they had definitely been on a roll and that I was very disappointed that they'd been denied the opportunity of putting their progress to the test against the Springboks pack in the quarter-finals. In particular I expressed my appreciation of the fact that they had so readily taken instructions – and sometimes criticism – from me for, after all, for many of them, I had been a fellow player only two seasons ago.

In the meantime Roger Lewis had called a meeting with all members of the coaching team, along with David Pickering.

Nigel, Rowland, Neil, Mark Bennett and myself turned up to find Gareth already there and looking quite dejected. We were then informed that Gareth was no longer the National Coach. We, as coaches, had an emotional few minutes on our own, during which we tried to come to terms with how suddenly and hurriedly the decision to dismiss Gareth had been made, before proceeding to the team room, where Roger Lewis announced to the squad that Gareth had been dismissed. The players looked on in disbelief, not being able to take in the fact that that decision had been taken so suddenly. Gareth, with great difficulty, addressed the squad briefly, and that was it. In no time we were all on the team bus and on our way to the airport. It was one of the quietest journeys that I had ever been on, with most of the party trying to get their heads around the events of the last two days.

We left Rhoose airport via a side exit, in order to avoid the large press contingent that awaited our party, prior to arriving back at the Vale Hotel. I then witnessed one of the saddest sights I had ever experienced in rugby when Gareth Jenkins, in order to avoid the attention of the press, raised his hand to bid us all farewell and walked off the bus before it arrived at the hotel forecourt. That was it. That someone who had given so much to Welsh rugby was forced to depart in such an ignominious manner was hard to believe. A week later Roger Lewis met with the coaching team to confirm that no major decisions would be made until Gareth's replacement had been appointed, except that Nigel would head the existing team during the preparations for the game against South Africa, towards the end of November.

# CHAPTER 18

# No Regrets

Anyone who takes himself too seriously always runs the
risk of looking ridiculous; anyone who can consistently laugh at
himself does not.

**Vaclav Havel**

I HAVE ALWAYS felt very privileged to be able to pursue a career
that has given me so much satisfaction in a sport that gives
so many people such pleasure. I would not have changed my
days as a player in any way whatsoever, despite my bitter
experiences at the outset when I spent so much time sitting
on the bench. Ironically, I think I eventually profited from
those experiences and they worked in my favour! I am now
fully aware of how a young player feels when he's placed in a
similar position. I don't know whether I could be a comfort to
such a person – since I myself felt at the time that I could not
have been consoled by anyone, but perhaps I could persuade
him that he shouldn't believe that everyone else is at fault
except himself!

My pursuit of a career in rugby has meant sacrifice on many
counts, particularly in the beginning when I lived in north Wales.
But perhaps the word 'choice' would be more appropriate than
'sacrifice', since it was my decision to take the path that I did
and since I was never forced to do anything against my will. My
family, however, had to pay a price as a result of my 'choices'. My
parents, particularly my father, who drove thousands of miles
in the early days to transport me to Mold, and later to south
Wales, and then hurried back to get to his work, or to keep a
preaching engagement, the following day. And latterly Tina and
the children, who have, and still are, obliged to arrange their

holidays and their lives around the demands of rugby.

As for myself, I would love to continue coaching. I have really enjoyed working with the Welsh forwards, seeing them develop both as individuals and as a pack. I also feel that my experiences with the national squad during the last sixteen months or so will serve me in good stead for the future, wherever it takes me. The task of being in charge of a pack and being able to organise and operate in the set pieces in accordance with my vision really appeals to me and I very much hope that, despite impending changes to the coaching set up of the national team, I'll be able to enjoy more of the same for many years to come, at whatever level.

Currently, there is a lot of uncertainty surrounding the future, but we know as a coaching group that we will be there for one last match, against a team that we should have faced in the quarter-finals of the World Cup – South Africa. Playing against the World Champions provides a great challenge for us, and one that we are all looking forward to; after all, we've beaten both the second-place and third-placed teams in the world during the last six months! As a pack we were frustrated that we were unable to use against them the momentum that we had generated in the Pool matches, and we will have to try and rediscover that rhythm quickly in the few remaining sessions now available to us.

In the meantime we have visited all the regional coaches to present them with a debrief of the World Cup and an analysis of the performance of each individual member from their region. I was able to share with those coaches the nature of the work I had been doing with their players, and was also able to see the training they were doing with them. Discussing the players and finding out about the role they play at the regional level is essential for me as I would not be meeting the Welsh forwards again until the Sunday before the Springbok match. I only hope that we are lucky with injuries in the European Cup fixtures in the weekends leading up to the match, and that we are able to select our preferred side.

At the moment there are many suggestions as to what should be done to improve the game in Wales, and if we are to make our mark again at international level there's no doubt that there needs to be changes in the structure in order to give us the best chance possible. We all want our regions to be successful as well as our national team and being that we only have a limited pool of players in Wales we need to look after them all – from the top, right down to the grass roots.

The success of the national team relies heavily on the strength of its foundations, and we need to improve our depth in strength in order to maintain a  healthy game. By that, I mean that we can not allow a 'comfort zone' to develop around our top players simply because there aren't enough players fighting for the same position. If it becomes too easy for our players to stay in the game and get paid for it, at whatever level, then we are in trouble. If the talent isn't coming through, then the only alternative for the regions, if they want to be successful, is to look elsewhere and bring in overseas players – and who can blame them? The knock-on effect from this would be a decreased number of players playing at the highest standard, and thereby limiting our selection, therefore ensuring that our academies are producing quality players for our regions is crucial. Those players then need to be seen at a high enough standard for them to be considered for selection by the regional coaches so that they will then play at a higher level. This means that the standard of our Premiership Division needs to be high enough to provide this environment. The Premiership in turn depends on the clubs below them and so on, all the way down through our divisions.

There are a number of examples of players that have come through our academy systems and who are now playing for their country and I have no doubt that if we can bring more of that talent through to the highest level, then the future will be one we can all look forward to. In the current climate it is very easy to overlook some of these positives but I am convinced that we have enough talent in Wales to be successful; we just need to pull together. This includes the media, who have a big part to play. I'm realistic enough not to expect to hear and read positive remarks all the time, but the present negativity with which we are surrounded is undermining a lot of good work that is currently being done. We are a small nation and we can ill afford to be spending our time fighting against each other, otherwise we will never make ground on the leading rugby nations. Wales is renowned for its choirs and its singing and if we are to be successful, we need to show some of that harmony both on and off the rugby field.

I have used some quotes that I thought were appropriate at the beginning of each chapter and as this is the last chapter I think it is only appropriate to finish with one that we all know and sometimes forget.

Failing to put things into perspective can happen to all of us at some time or other, but when I hear some of the comments being shouted at young children playing rugby on a Sunday morning and when I reflect on the year that's just gone, I'm reminded of it – it's only a game!

We publish a wide range of books of Welsh interest in both languages. For a full list of publications, please ask for a copy of our new, free catalogue – or you may surf into our website

**www.ylolfa.com**

where you may order books on-line.

TALYBONT CEREDIGION CYMRU SY24 5HE
*email* ylolfa@ylolfa.com
*website* www.ylolfa.com
*tel* 01970 832 304
*fax* 832 782